MASTERING DATA STRUCTURES: ALGORITHMS AND APPLICATIONS

ISHWARYA M.V
SHARMILA.L
JAYASHREE ANANTH.S
MOHANA PRIYA.P

Made with ♥ on the Notion Press Platform
www.notionpress.com

Contents

CHAPTER ONE

ABSTRACT DATA TYPES

Abstract Data Types (ADTs) represent a core principle in computer science, characterizing a data structure solely based on its functionality as perceived by the user, rather than its underlying implementation. Consequently, an ADT delineates the permissible operations on the data type and the kinds of data that can be accommodated, while refraining from providing specifics regarding the implementation of these operations.

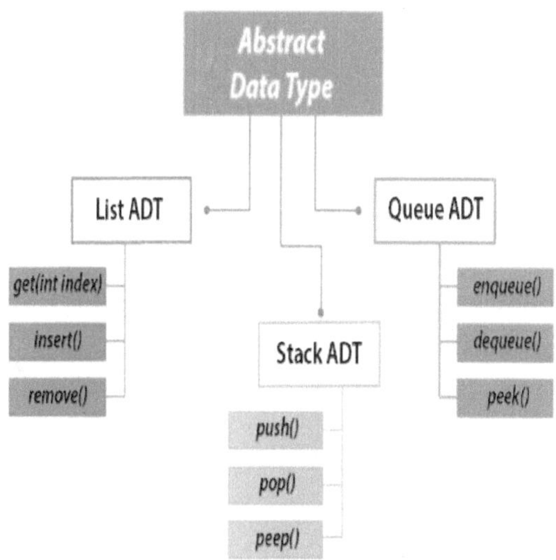

ADT classification

Key Characteristics of ADTs:

1. **Encapsulation**: ADTs encapsulate data and the operations that manipulate that data, hiding the implementation details from the user.
2. **Interface**: Abstract Data Types (ADTs) offer a well-defined interface that specifies a collection of operations (methods) applicable to the data type, including the addition, removal, or retrieval of elements.
3. **Implementation Independence:** Users of an ADT focus solely on its usage rather than its underlying implementation. This characteristic enables various implementations, such as linked lists or arrays, to be interchanged without impacting the code that interacts with the

ADT.**Common Examples of ADTs:**

1. **Stack:**

    - **Operations**: push, pop, peek, isEmpty
    - **Behavior**: Last-In-First-Out (LIFO)

2. **Queue:**

    - **Operations**: enqueue, dequeue, peek, isEmpty
    - **Behavior**: First-In-First-Out (FIFO)

3. **List:**

    - **Operations**: insert, delete, get, set, size
    - **Behavior**: Ordered collection of items

4. **Set:**

- **Operations**: add, remove, contains, size
- **Behavior**: Collection of unique items

5. **Map (or Dictionary)**:

   - **Operations**: put, get, remove, containsKey, size
   - **Behavior**: Key-value pairs

Advantages of Using ADTs:

- **Modularity**: Facilitates modular programming, allowing developers to build and maintain systems more easily.
- **Reusability**: ADTs can be reused across different programs and projects.
- **Ease of Maintenance**: Changes in the underlying implementation do not affect the code that uses the ADT.

Key Aspects Of Encapsulation:

1. **Data Hiding:**

- Encapsulation conceals the internal state of an object from external entities. Users engage with the data solely through clearly defined interfaces (methods), thereby restricting direct access to the data fields.
- This approach safeguards the integrity of the data by allowing modifications only through regulated means.

1. **Controlled Access**:

   - Encapsulation allows for the implementation of access modifiers (like public, private, and protected in many programming languages) to control how data can be accessed or modified.

2. **Interface Definition:**

- An Abstract Data Type (ADT) establishes a distinct interface that outlines the operations accessible to the user, while concealing the underlying implementation specifics.
- This approach simplifies the comprehension and utilization of the data type, as users are required only to understand how to invoke the methods, rather than the internal workings of those methods.

4. Flexibility in Implementation:

The internal mechanisms of an Abstract Data Type (ADT) are concealed, allowing for modifications in the implementation without impacting the end users.

5. Enhanced Maintainability:

Encapsulation contributes to the ease of maintenance and debugging of code. When a problem occurs, developers can concentrate on the methods specified in the interface, without the necessity of delving into the intricacies of the implementation.

Interface in Abstract Data Types (ADTs):

In the realm of Abstract Data Types (ADTs), an interface delineates a collection of operations (methods) that can be executed on the data type, clarifying the functionalities that the ADT offers to users. It serves as a formal agreement that specifies how the data type can be utilized, while keeping the underlying implementation hidden.

Key Features of Interfaces in ADTs:

1. **Specification of Operations:**

    - The interface clearly defines all available operations that can be performed on the ADT. For instance, for a Stack ADT, the interface might include methods like push, pop, peek, and isEmpty.

Specification of Operations in Abstract Data Types (ADTs):

The operational specifications within Abstract Data Types (ADTs) delineate the collection of methods or functions applicable to the data type. This specification details the functionality of each operation, the parameters required, and the expected return values, while concealing the intricacies of the underlying implementation.

Key Aspects of Specification of Operations:

Input and Output:

- The specification includes details about the types and constraints of inputs and outputs. For example, in a Stack ADT, the push operation may take an element of type T as input, while the pop operation returns an element of type T.

Behavioral Expectations:

- The specification should define the expected behavior of each operation, including edge cases. For instance, it should specify what happens if a pop operation is called on an empty stack (e.g., returning None or raising an error).

Preconditions and Postconditions:

- It can be helpful to specify preconditions (conditions that must be true before an operation is called) and postconditions (conditions that must be true after an operation is completed). This adds a layer of robustness and helps prevent misuse.

Complexity Information:

- In certain applications, it can be beneficial to provide details regarding the time and space complexity of operations. This information enables users to comprehend the performance consequences of utilizing the Abstract Data Type (ADT) in various scenarios.

Example of Operation Specification:

- Consider a List ADT with the following operations:

Insert:

- **Signature**: insert(index: int, element: T) -> None
- **Precondition:** 0 <= index <= size of the list
- **Delete:**
- **Signature**: delete(index: int) -> T
- **Description**: Removes and returns the element at the specified index. Raises IndexError if the index is out of bounds.
- **Get:**
- **Signature**: get(index: int) -> T
- **Precondition:** 0 <= index < size of the list
- **Postcondition**: The list remains unchanged.
- **Size:**
- **Signature**: size() -> int
- **Precondition**: None.
- **Postcondition**: None.

2. **No Implementation Details:**

   - The interface does not provide any information on how the operations are implemented. This allows for multiple implementations of the same interface, providing flexibility to choose or change implementations without affecting users.

No Implementation Details in Abstract Data Types (ADTs)

- The principle of **no implementation details** in Abstract Data Types (ADTs) emphasizes that users should interact with the data type solely through its specified interface, without needing to know how the operations are implemented. This separation of interface and implementation is essential for several reasons.

Key Aspects of "No Implementation Details":

User-Focused Interaction:

Users are able to concentrate on utilizing the Abstract Data Type (ADT) without the need to concern themselves with its underlying construction. This approach enhances the user experience, facilitating the learning and application of the data type across different scenarios.

Flexibility of Implementation:

It is possible to have several implementations of the same ADT without altering the interface. For instance, a Stack ADT may be realized through either an array or a linked list. Users have the option to select an implementation based on performance or memory requirements, all while keeping their code intact.

Ease of Maintenance and Upgrades:

- Changes to the implementation (like optimizing algorithms or switching data structures) can be made without affecting the code that relies on the ADT. This means that developers can enhance performance or fix bugs without requiring changes from users.

Promotes Abstraction:

- Hiding implementation details encourages abstraction, allowing developers to think about the high-level operations rather than the specifics of how they are carried out. This leads to cleaner and more modular code.

Example of No Implementation Details:

- Consider a Set ADT. The interface might specify operations like add, remove, and contains, but it does not reveal whether the underlying implementation uses a hash table, a balanced tree, or a simple array.

Multiple Implementations:

Hash Set: This implementation uses a hash table for fast lookups and insertions.

Tree Set: This implementation uses a balanced binary tree to maintain sorted order.

Array Set: This implementation uses a dynamic array, but operations may be less efficient due to linear searches.

In all cases, users of the Set ADT will interact with the same interface without needing to know or care about the underlying implementation details. They can add or remove elements, check for membership, and get the size of the set without understanding whether it uses a hash table or a tree structure.

3. **User-Centric Design**:

   - Interfaces are designed with the user in mind. They focus on what operations are necessary for the user rather than how those operations are carried out.

User-Centric Design in Abstract Data Types (ADTs)

- **User-centric design** in the context of Abstract Data Types (ADTs) emphasizes creating interfaces and operations that are intuitive and easy to use for the developer or end user. This approach ensures that the data type is accessible and meets the needs of its users while abstracting away unnecessary complexities.

Key Aspects of User-Centric Design:
Intuitive Interfaces:

- The operations provided by the ADT should be named and structured in a way that reflects their functionality, making it easier for users to understand what each operation does. For instance, a push method on a Stack ADT clearly indicates that an element is being added.
- **Clear Documentation:**
- Comprehensive documentation is crucial. It should describe the purpose of the ADT, detail each operation's behavior, provide usage examples, and outline any preconditions or postconditions. Good documentation helps users quickly grasp how to effectively use the ADT.
- **Consistency:**
- The naming conventions and operation signatures should be consistent across different ADTs. For example, if one data structure uses add to insert an element, another similar structure should ideally use the same terminology. This consistency reduces the learning curve for users familiar with other ADTs.
- **Error Handling:**
- User-centric design should include sensible error handling. When operations fail (e.g., popping from an empty stack), the behavior should be predictable and well-defined, such as raising an appropriate exception. This helps users understand what went wrong and how to fix it.

Performance Considerations:

It is essential to prioritize usability; however, one must also take into account the performance implications. Users ought to understand the time and space complexity associated with various operations, which will empower them to make informed choices tailored to their individual requirements.

User-Centric Features:

- **Intuitive Operation Names:** The methods clearly indicate their purpose (e.g., enqueue, dequeue).
- **Documentation:** Each method includes a docstring that explains its function and any exceptions it may raise.
- **Consistent Return Types:** Methods like is_empty and size return boolean and integer values, respectively, making the behavior predictable.
- **Error Handling:** The dequeue and peek methods raise exceptions when called on an empty queue, informing users of misuse

1. **Consistency and Predictability:**

- A well-defined interface ensures that users can reliably interact with the ADT. They know what to expect from the available methods, leading to more intuitive use of the data type.
- **Key Aspects of Consistency and Predictability:**

Uniform Naming Conventions:

- Consistent terminology for operations across various Abstract Data Types (ADTs) facilitates users in swiftly acquiring knowledge and retaining the functions. For instance, if the method for inserting an element is designated as add in a Set ADT, it should preferably be referred to as add in other collections such as List or Map.

Similar Behavior Across Data Types:

- ADTs that serve similar purposes should exhibit similar behaviors. For instance, a pop operation in both a Stack and a Queue should logically remove an element, even though they operate differently (LIFO vs. FIFO). This allows users to transfer their understanding from one ADT to another.

- **Defined Error Handling:**
- Predictable error handling is crucial. When a user performs an invalid operation (e.g., removing an item from an empty data structure), the response should be consistent, such as raising a specific type of exception. This predictability allows users to anticipate outcomes and handle errors gracefully in their code.
- **Clear Operation Contracts:**
- Each operation should have a well-defined contract, specifying what the operation does, its input parameters, and its output. Users should know exactly what to expect when they call a method. For example, the size method of a List ADT should consistently return the current number of elements.
- **Performance Characteristics:**
- Users should have predictable performance characteristics for the operations of an ADT. For instance, if insert is O(n) in one implementation of a List ADT, users can anticipate that it will generally be O(n) across similar lists unless otherwise noted.
- **Example of Consistency and Predictability:**

A Stack Abstract Data Type (ADT) can be defined with the following consistent operations:

Consistent Features:

- **Naming**: All operations use clear, standard names (push, pop, peek), which are commonly understood by users familiar with stack concepts.
- **Error Handling**: The pop and peek methods consistently raise exceptions when the stack is empty, making error responses predictable.
- **Operation Contracts**: Each method provides a clear contract about its behavior, inputs, and outputs, ensuring users know what to expect.

3. **Polymorphism:**

   Dynamic Method Dispatch:

   - In languages that support polymorphism, the appropriate method implementation is determined at runtime. This means that the method called depends on the actual object type, allowing for more flexible and dynamic code.
   - **Simplified Code Maintenance:**
   - Changes to implementations do not require changes to the code that uses the ADT. If a new implementation of an interface is added, existing code can leverage it without modification, improving maintainability.
   - **Enhanced Flexibility:**
   - Polymorphism allows for more flexible architectures. Developers can easily swap out one implementation for another, such as switching from a stack implemented with an array to one implemented with a linked list, without changing the code that uses it.

Key Features of Implementation Independence:

Separation of Interface and Implementation in Abstract Data Types (ADTs):

The distinction between interface and implementation is a core principle in the design of Abstract Data Types (ADTs). This principle highlights the importance of the interface. (the set of operations and methods exposed to users) should be distinct from the implementation (the underlying code and data structures that perform the operations). This separation provides numerous benefits, enhancing flexibility, maintainability, and usability.

Key Aspects of Separation of Interface and Implementation:

1. **Encapsulation:**

- By separating the interface from the implementation, the internal workings of the ADT are hidden from users. This encapsulation protects the integrity of the data and prevents users from directly manipulating it, reducing the risk of errors.

2. **Ease of Maintenance and Updates:**

   - Changes to the implementation can be made without affecting users, as long as the interface remains unchanged. This means that developers can optimize, refactor, or improve the implementation without requiring modifications to the code that uses the ADT.

3. **Enhanced Code Reusability:**

   - By relying on interfaces, developers can reuse the same code with different implementations. This is particularly useful in large systems where different modules might need to use the same ADT but with different performance characteristics.

4. **Improved Testing and Debugging:**

   - With a clear separation, testing becomes more straightforward. You can test the implementation independently from the interface, allowing for isolated debugging and ensuring that changes in one part do not inadvertently break another.

Flexibility in Implementation of Abstract Data Types (ADTs): The ability to implement Abstract Data Types (ADTs) with flexibility is a significant benefit. This concept permits various implementations of a single ADT interface, allowing developers to select or modify implementations according to particular requirements, performance factors, or the context of the application.

Key Aspects of Flexibility in Implementation:

1. **Multiple Data Structures:**

A Queue ADT may be constructed with an array, a linked list, or a circular buffer. **Performance Optimization:**

- Different implementations can optimize for different performance metrics. For example, one implementation might prioritize speed for insertion and deletion, while another may prioritize memory usage or maintain order. This allows developers to tailor the ADT to the specific performance requirements of their applications.

2. **Ease of Replacement:**

    - When the implementation of an ADT needs to change (for example, to improve efficiency or adapt to new requirements), the code that uses the ADT remains unchanged as long as the interface is preserved. This decoupling makes it easier to replace or upgrade implementations without impacting the broader system.

3. **Specialized Implementations:**

    - Developers can create specialized versions of an ADT for specific applications. For instance, a Set ADT could have a hash-based implementation for fast lookups or a tree-based implementation for ordered elements. This allows for optimization based on the specific usage patterns of the data type.

4. **Interoperability:**

- Flexible implementations enable different parts of a system to interact seamlessly. For example, if one module of a program requires a thread-safe version of a stack, a different implementation can be provided without changing how other modules interact with the stack.

5. **Adaptation to Evolving Requirements:**

    - As application requirements change, the ability to switch implementations allows developers to adapt the data type to new needs. For example, if an application starts handling larger datasets, a more efficient implementation can be adopted without overhauling the entire codebase.

Changes to the implementation (e.g., optimizing algorithms or switching data structures) do not affect the code that uses the ADT. This encapsulation allows for easier maintenance and adaptation of software over time, as developers can improve implementations without breaking existing code.

Ease of Modification and Maintenance in Abstract Data Types (ADTs):

Ease of modification and maintenance is a crucial advantage of using Abstract Data Types (ADTs) in software development. By separating the interface from the implementation, ADTs allow developers to make changes to the underlying code with minimal impact on the rest of the application. This principle leads to more robust, flexible, and maintainable codebases.

Key Aspects of Ease of Modification and Maintenance:

1. **Encapsulation of Implementation Details:**

    - Since the implementation details are hidden from the user, changes can be made to the internal workings of the ADT without affecting how it is used in other parts of the program. This encapsulation allows developers to refactor or optimize the implementation while keeping the interface intact.

2. **Consistent Interfaces:**
   - Because the interface remains consistent, modifications to the implementation do not require changes to the code that interacts with the ADT. Users of the ADT can continue to rely on the same method signatures and behaviors, reducing the risk of introducing bugs.
3. **Simplified Upgrades:**
   - When new features or enhancements are needed, developers can add them to the ADT without altering existing functionality. This is particularly beneficial in large systems, where maintaining backward compatibility is essential.
4. **Isolation of Changes:**
   - Modifications can be isolated to specific implementations. For example, if a new algorithm is introduced to improve performance, it can be implemented in a new class that adheres to the same interface, leaving existing implementations and their users unaffected.
5. **Testing and Debugging:**
   - The separation of interface and implementation simplifies testing. Each implementation can be tested independently, ensuring that modifications do not break existing functionality. This isolation aids in debugging, making it easier to identify and fix issues.
6. **Adaptability to Evolving Requirements:**

- As application needs change, the ability to modify or replace implementations enables developers to adapt the ADT to new requirements without a complete rewrite of the codebase.

Implementation independence encourages the reuse of ADTs across different projects or components. Since the interface remains constant, developers can easily switch between different implementations based on their needs without rewriting code that uses the ADT.

Promotes Reusability in Abstract Data Types (ADTs):

Reusability is one of the key benefits of using Abstract Data Types (ADTs) in software development.

Key Aspects of Promoting Reusability:

1. **Standardized Interfaces:**
    - ADTs provide standardized interfaces that define a set of operations. Once an interface is established, any implementation adhering to that interface can be used interchangeably. This allows developers to leverage existing code without needing to rewrite functionality.
2. **Decoupled Code:**
    - The separation of interface and implementation ensures that code using an ADT does not depend on the specific details of how the ADT is implemented. This decoupling means that changes to the implementation do not affect the code that relies on the ADT, making it easier to reuse components in different contexts.
3. **Flexible Implementations:**
    - Different implementations of the same ADT can be created for various needs (e.g., performance, memory usage).

4. **Modularity:**
   - ADTs promote a modular design, where components can be developed and tested independently. This modularity makes it easier to identify reusable components that can be integrated into different systems or applications without modification.

5. **Encouragement of Best Practices:**
   - By defining clear interfaces, ADTs encourage developers to adhere to best practices in software design. This not only enhances code quality but also increases the likelihood that reusable components are robust, well-tested, and easy to integrate.

6. **Libraries and Frameworks:**
   - ADTs are foundational in many libraries and frameworks, allowing developers to leverage well-designed data structures and algorithms without having to implement them from scratch. This accelerates development and fosters code sharing among developers.

3. **Encourages Abstraction:**
   - By focusing on the interface and ignoring implementation details, developers can think more abstractly about data types. This abstraction simplifies problem-solving and design, allowing for a focus on higher-level concepts.

Encourages Abstraction in Abstract Data Types (ADTs)

Abstraction is a fundamental principle in software design that focuses on hiding complex implementation details while exposing only the essential features of a system. Abstract Data Types (ADTs) are designed to promote abstraction, allowing developers to work with high-level representations of data structures without needing to understand their internal workings. This leads to clearer, more maintainable code.

Key Aspects of Abstraction in ADTs:

1. **Simplified Interaction**:
   - ADTs provide a simplified interface for users, allowing them to interact with complex data structures through a well-defined set of operations. Users do not need to know how these operations are implemented, which reduces cognitive load.
2. **Focus on High-Level Design**:
   - By abstracting away implementation details, developers can concentrate on high-level design and functionality. This helps in designing systems that meet user requirements without getting bogged down by low-level concerns.
3. **Improved Code Readability**:
   - Abstraction enhances code readability by allowing developers to use intuitive method names and interfaces that clearly describe their purpose. This makes it easier for others (or even the original developer at a later time) to understand the code.
4. **Easier Collaboration**:
   - When working in teams, abstraction allows different team members to focus on different parts of the system. One person can work on the implementation of an ADT, while others can focus on integrating it into the larger system

without needing to understand the intricacies of its implementation.

5. **Facilitates Change:**

    ◦ Since users interact with an ADT through its interface, changes to the implementation do not affect the code that uses it as long as the interface remains the same. This makes it easier to modify or replace components as requirements evolve.

6. **Encourages Modular Design:**

    ◦ Abstraction supports modular design by promoting the creation of self-contained components. Each ADT can be developed, tested, and maintained independently, leading to cleaner and more organized codebases.

Abstraction Benefits:

- **Simplified Interaction**: Users interact with the GraphInterface without needing to know how the graph is stored or manipulated.
- **Focus on High-Level Design**: Developers can focus on how to use graphs in their applications without worrying about the underlying data structure.
- **Improved Readability**: The clear interface makes it easy to understand what operations are available and what they do.

Example of Implementation Independence:

Consider the Queue ADT mentioned earlier. The interface specifies methods like enqueue, dequeue, and peek. There could be various implementations:

1. **Linked List Queue:**

- This implementation uses a linked list, where nodes represent elements in the queue. Operations are performed by adding or removing nodes.

A linked list queue is a data structure that uses a linked list to implement the queue functionality. A queue operates on a first-in, first-out (FIFO) principle, meaning that the first element added to the queue will be the first one to be removed.

Key Components

Circular Buffer Queue:

This implementation uses a circular buffer to optimize space and allow for efficient wrapping of the indices.

In each case, the user interacts with the same interface, regardless of which implementation is used. For instance, the following code could work with any of the implementations without changes:

```
python
def process_queue(queue: QueueInterface):
queue.enqueue("item1")
item = queue.dequeue()
print(item)
```

A circular buffer queue, commonly referred to as a ring buffer, is a data structure of fixed size that employs a circular array to facilitate queue operations. This design promotes efficient space utilization by wrapping around upon reaching the buffer's end..

Key Concepts

1. **Fixed Size**: The buffer has a maximum size defined at initialization, which limits how many elements it can hold.

Fixed Size in Array-Based Queue:

A **fixed size** refers to the pre-defined maximum capacity of an array-based queue. This means that once the queue is created, it cannot dynamically resize to accommodate more elements beyond its specified limit. Understanding fixed size is crucial for implementing and managing an array-based queue effectively.

Key Characteristics of Fixed Size:

1. **Capacity Limitation:**
   - The queue has a specific capacity determined at the time of its creation.
2. **Memory Allocation:**
   - Memory for the array is allocated statically (at compile time) or dynamically (at runtime) based on the specified capacity. However, the size remains constant throughout the queue's lifetime.
3. **Overflow Condition:**
   - When the queue reaches its maximum capacity and an attempt is made to enqueue an additional element, an overflow condition occurs. This situation must be handled gracefully, usually by raising an exception or providing an error message.
4. **Simplicity:**
   - The implementation of a fixed-size queue is simpler than that of a dynamically sized queue, making it easier to understand and manage.

How Circular Buffers Work:

1. **Array Representation:** A circular buffer is implemented using a fixed-size array. When the buffer is full and elements are

dequeued, the space becomes available again for new elements.

2. **Maintaining Indices**:
   - **Front Pointer**: Indicates where the next element will be dequeued from.
   - **Rear Pointer**: Indicates where the next element will be added.
   - Both pointers use modulo arithmetic with the buffer's capacity to ensure they stay within bounds.

Pointers in the Context of Data Structures:

Pointers are fundamental concepts in programming, particularly when working with data structures like linked lists, trees, and graphs. They are variables that store the memory address of another variable, allowing for dynamic data management and manipulation. In the context of data structures, pointers enable efficient linking of nodes and facilitate operations like insertion, deletion, and traversal.

Key Characteristics of Pointers:

1. **Memory Addressing**:
   - Pointers hold the address of another variable or data structure, enabling programs to reference and manipulate data in memory without duplicating it.

2. **Dynamic Memory Allocation**:
   - Pointers are often used in conjunction with dynamic memory allocation, allowing for flexible data structures that can grow and shrink as needed.

3. **Efficient Operations**:

- The operations can be performed without shifting elements, unlike in array-based structures.

4. **Complex Data Structures:**

   - They enable the creation of relationships between nodes, allowing for hierarchical and non-linear data representations.

Operations

1. **Enqueue:** Add an element to the rear of the queue.

The **enqueue** operation in a circular buffer queue is responsible for adding an element to the rear of the queue. Here's a detailed explanation of how it works, along with the implementation:

Enqueue Operation Steps:

1. **Check for Fullness:** Before adding an element, the function checks if the queue is full. If it is, an error is raised (e.g., an exception) because no more elements can be added until some are dequeued.
2. **Add the Element:** If there is space, the element is placed at the position indicated by the rear pointer.
3. **Update the Rear Pointer:** The rear pointer is then incremented. If it reaches the end of the buffer (the maximum capacity), it wraps around to the beginning of the array using modulo arithmetic.
4. **Increment Size:** The size of the queue is increased by one to reflect the addition of the new element.

Key Points

- **Complexity:** The enqueue operation runs in O(1) time, making it efficient.

- **Capacity Check**: It's crucial to check if the queue is full to avoid overwriting existing data.
- **Circular Behavior**: The use of modulo ensures that when the rear pointer exceeds the array bounds, it wraps back to the start.

The **dequeue** operation in a circular buffer queue is responsible for removing and returning the element at the front of the queue. Here's a detailed explanation of how it works, along with the implementation:

Dequeue Operation Steps

1. **Retrieve the Element**: If the queue is not empty, the element at the front pointer is retrieved for return.
2. **Update the Front Pointer**: The front pointer is then incremented. If it reaches the end of the buffer (the maximum capacity), it wraps around to the beginning of the array using modulo arithmetic.

Key Points:

- **Complexity**: The dequeue operation runs in O(1) time, making it very efficient.
- **Circular Behavior**: Using modulo arithmetic ensures that the front pointer wraps around correctly, maintaining the circular structure.

3. Peek:

Retrieve the element located at the front of the queue without removing it.

```
queue = [1, 2, 3]
front_element = queue[0] # Access the front element
```

4. Is Empty:

- The is_empty function in a circular buffer queue serves to ascertain if there are any elements present in the queue. This function is essential to avoid errors that may arise when attempting to dequeue from an empty queue. Below are the steps involved in this operation, along with an example implementation:

Is Empty Operation Steps:

1. Assess Size: The most straightforward method to check if the queue is empty is by evaluating the size attribute. If the size equals zero, the queue is considered empty.

2. Return Boolean: The function will yield True if the queue is empty and False if it contains elements.

Key Points:

- **Efficiency**: The is_empty operation runs in O(1) time, making it very efficient to check the queue's state.
- **Usage**: This operation is often used before dequeueing to ensure that the queue has elements to remove, preventing runtime errors.

Is Full: Check if the queue is full.

The "is full" operation checks whether a queue has reached its maximum capacity. This is particularly relevant for fixed-size queues, like those implemented with arrays.

Considerations

- In dynamic implementations (like linked lists), queues are rarely "full" unless system memory is exhausted.
- For circular queues, you'd typically check if the next position of rear equals front.

Classes:

1. Definition: A class functions as a template for generating objects in OOP. It integrates data and the methods that manipulate that data.**Characteristics**:

Attributes:

Data members that hold the state of an object.

Attributes, often referred to as data members or properties, are fundamental components of a class in object-oriented programming. They represent the state or characteristics of an object created from that class. Here's a deeper look at attributes:

Key Points about Attributes:

1. Definition: Attributes refer to the variables associated with a class. They store data that is particular to each instance (object) of that class.

1. **Initialization**: Attributes are typically initialized in the class's constructor (e.g., __init__ in Python). This allows each object to set its own initial state.

Methods:

Functions that are established within the class and have the ability to modify the object's state.

Methods are functions defined within a class that operate on the attributes of an object. They allow for interaction with the object's state and provide the behavior associated with that object. Here's a closer look at methods:

Key Points about Methods

1. **Definition**: Methods are functions that belong to a class. They can access and modify the object's attributes, enabling the manipulation of its state.
2. **Types of Methods**:

- Instance Methods are the most prevalent type, functioning on the attributes of an instance. They necessitate an instance of the class for invocation and generally accept 'self' as the initial parameter to denote the instance.
- Class Methods, on the other hand, work with class attributes and are designated with the @classmethod decorator. These methods take 'cls' as the first parameter, which refers to the class

itself.

3. **Accessing Attributes**: Methods can read and modify both instance and class attributes. This encapsulation allows for a controlled interface for interacting with the object's state.
4. **Example**: Here's a simple class demonstrating various methods:

Key Points about Inheritance:

1. **Benefits**:
   - **Code Reuse**: Common functionality can be defined in a superclass and reused in subclasses, reducing redundancy.
   - **Hierarchical Organization**: Classes can be organized in a hierarchy, making it easier to understand relationships and functionality.
   - **Polymorphism**: Subclasses can override methods from the superclass, allowing for dynamic behavior based on the object's actual type.
2. **Types of Inheritance**:
   - **Single Inheritance**: A subclass inherits from one superclass.
   - **Multiple Inheritance**: A subclass inherits from multiple superclasses (supported in languages like Python, but can introduce complexity).
   - **Multilevel Inheritance**: A class derives from a class that is itself a subclass of another class.
   - **Hierarchical Inheritance**: Multiple subclasses inherit from a single superclass.
3. **Example**: Here's an example illustrating inheritance:
4. **Method Overriding**: In the example, both Dog and Cat override the speak method from the Animal class to provide their specific

implementations.

Polymorphism:
Key Points about Polymorphism

1. **Definition**: Polymorphism allows methods to be called on objects of different classes that share a common interface, meaning they can be treated uniformly despite their different implementations.
2. **Benefits**:
    - **Code Flexibility**: Allows for writing more general and reusable code.
    - **Interface Implementation**: Different classes can implement the same interface in different ways, promoting a more abstract design.
3. **Example**: Here's a simple illustration of polymorphism using method overriding:
4. **Dynamic Behavior**: In the example, the print_area function calls the area method on different Shape objects. Even though rectangle and circle are of different classes, they are treated as instances of Shape, showcasing polymorphism.

Relationship Between ADTs and Classes:

- **Implementation**: A class can be used to implement an ADT. The class defines the specific details of how the operations are carried out, while the ADT specifies the operations abstractly.
- **Design**: When designing software, you often start with the ADT to determine what behaviors are needed, then implement those behaviors using classes.

The relationship between Abstract Data Types (ADTs) and classes is fundamental in object-oriented programming, as both concepts serve to define and structure data and behaviors in software design. Here's an overview of their relationship:

Key Relationships Between ADTs and Classes

1. **Conceptual vs. Implementation**:
   - **ADTs**: Represent a conceptual model that defines a data type by its behavior and operations (e.g., stack, queue, list) without specifying how these operations are implemented.
   - **Classes**: Provide the actual implementation of ADTs in a programming language.
2. **Encapsulation**:
   - Both ADTs and classes promote encapsulation, allowing the internal workings (data and implementation details) to be hidden while exposing a well-defined interface for interaction. This means users of the ADT or class can perform operations without needing to understand the underlying details.
3. **Interface Definition**:
   - An ADT outlines the set of operations and expected behaviors, which can be translated into methods within a class. The class implements these operations, providing concrete functionality.
4. **Abstraction**:
   - Classes take this abstraction and provide the specific implementation, enabling developers to work at different levels of detail.

5. **Example**: Consider a simple ADT for a stack:
   - **ADT Specification**:
     - Operations: push(item), pop(), peek(), is_empty()

Key Concepts of OOP:

1. **Objects**:

Definition:

- An object represents a particular instance of a class, encapsulating both data and behavior. It functions as an independent entity that contains attributes (data) and methods (functions) that specify the capabilities of the object.

1. **Attributes**:

- Attributes are the properties or characteristics of an object. They hold the state of the object. For instance, in a Car class, attributes might include color, make, and model.

2. **Real-World Representation**:

- Objects are designed to represent real-world entities or concepts. For example:
- A Dog object could represent a specific dog with attributes like breed and age, and methods like bark() and fetch().

3. **Encapsulation**:
   - Objects encapsulate their state and behavior, meaning that their internal data is hidden from the outside world. This allows for controlled access to attributes through methods,

promoting data integrity.

4. **Example**: Here's a simple Python example demonstrating an object:

```
Python
# Instantiating an object of the Automobile class
my_automobile = Automobile("Toyota", "Corolla", 2020)
# Accessing attributes and methods
print(f"My automobile is a {my_automobile.production_year} {my_automobile.manufacturer} {my_automobile.type}.")
print(my_automobile.ignite_engine()) # Output: Engine ignited
```

2. **Classes:**

A class serves as a template for generating objects. It outlines the characteristics (attributes) and functionalities (methods) that the objects instantiated from the class will possess. Classes enhance code reusability.

? **Structure of a Class:**

Attribute: Variables within a class are designated to maintain the state of an object. Each object created from the class possesses its own unique set of attribute values.

Methods: are functions established within a class that execute actions utilizing the class's attributes. They delineate the behavior of the objects.

? **Instantiation:**

- Creating an object from a class is known as instantiation. Each instance (object) of a class has its own unique set of attributes, but shares the same methods defined in the class.

? **Code Reusability:**

- Classes promote code reuse by allowing developers to define common attributes and methods once, and then create multiple objects that share this functionality. This reduces redundancy and improves maintainability.

? **Modularity**:

- By organizing code into classes, developers can break down complex systems into smaller, manageable components. Each class can be developed, tested, and maintained independently.

? **Inheritance**:

- Classes can inherit from other classes, allowing for the creation of a hierarchy. A subclass can inherit attributes and methods from a superclass, promoting code reuse and extending functionality.

? **Encapsulation**:

- Classes encapsulate the data and methods related to an object, allowing for a clear interface. This helps prevent unintended interference with the object's internal state modularity.

Encapsulation:

1. **Definition**:
    - Encapsulation is a fundamental concept in object-oriented programming that entails the combination of data (attributes) and the methods (functions) that manipulate that data into a unified entity referred to as an object. This principle facilitates the regulation of access to the internal state of an object.

2. **Data Hiding**:

    - Encapsulation promotes data hiding by restricting direct access to an object's attributes. This means that the internal state of an object cannot be modified directly from outside the object, which helps protect the integrity of the data. Instead, access to the data is provided through methods (getters and setters).

3. **Interface**:

    - An object exposes a well-defined interface, which is a set of public methods that allow interaction with the object. This interface enables users to perform operations on the object without needing to understand its internal workings.

4. **Benefits**:

    - **Improved Maintainability**: Changes to an object's internal implementation Modifications can be implemented without impacting external code that interacts with the object, provided that the interface remains unchanged.
    - **Increased Security**: By controlling access to the internal state, encapsulation helps prevent unintended interference or misuse of the object's data.
    - **Simplified Interaction**: Users are able to engage with the object through its public methods, facilitating usage without requiring knowledge of its internal architecture.

5. **Example**: Here is an illustration in Python that exemplifies the concept of encapsulation:
6. **Private Attributes**:

    - This designation restricts direct access from outside the class, thereby upholding the principle of encapsulation.

Abstraction

1. **Definition**:
    - Abstraction serves as a core principle in object-oriented programming, emphasizing the concealment of intricate realities while revealing only the essential components. This approach enables developers to streamline a system by creating classes that reflect fundamental attributes, thereby eliminating superfluous details.

2. **Purpose**:
    - The main goal of abstraction is to reduce complexity and increase efficiency in software development. By focusing on high-level operations and interactions, programmers can manage and understand systems more easily.

3. **How It Works**:
    - Abstraction can be achieved through the use of abstract classes and interfaces. An abstract class can define methods that must be implemented by subclasses, while interfaces provide a contract that implementing classes must follow.

4. **Benefits**:
    - **Simplified Code**: By hiding implementation details, abstraction makes code easier to read and maintain.
    - **Enhanced Flexibility**: Changes in implementation can be made without affecting the interface, allowing for easier updates and modifications.
    - **Improved Reusability**: Abstract classes and interfaces can be reused across different parts of a program or in different projects.

Inheritance

1. **Purpose:**
    - The main purpose of inheritance is to promote code reuse, reduce redundancy, and facilitate the creation of hierarchical relationships between classes. By allowing subclasses to inherit common functionality from superclasses, developers can create more organized and maintainable code.

2. **How It Works:**
    - When a subclass inherits from a superclass, it automatically gains access to the superclass's attributes and methods. The subclass can also override methods to provide specific functionality, while still retaining the characteristics of the superclass.

3. **Types of Inheritance:**
    - **Single Inheritance**: A subclass inherits from a single superclass.
    - **Multiple Inheritance**: A subclass inherits from multiple superclasses. (Note: This can lead to complexity and is not supported in all programming languages.)
    - **Multilevel Inheritance**: A subclass serves as a superclass for another subclass.
    - **Hierarchical Inheritance**: Multiple subclasses inherit from a single superclass.

4. **Benefits:**
    - **Code Reusability**: Common functionality can be defined in a superclass and reused in multiple subclasses.

- **Logical Structure**: Establishes a natural relationship between classes, making the codebase easier to understand.
- **Extensibility**: New subclasses can be created with minimal changes to existing code, allowing for easy extension of functionality.

5. **Example**: Here's a Python example demonstrating inheritance:

```
python
class Animal: # Superclass
def __init__(self, name):
self.name = name
def speak(self):
return "Some sound"
class Dog(Animal): # Subclass
def speak(self): # Method overriding
return "Woof!"
class Cat(Animal): # Subclass
def speak(self): # Method overriding
return "Meow!"
# Creating instances of the subclasses
dog = Dog("Buddy")
cat = Cat("Whiskers")
# Accessing methods
print(f"{dog.name}: {dog.speak()}") # Output: Buddy: Woof!
print(f"{cat.name}: {cat.speak()}") # Output: Whiskers: Meow!
```

Polymorphism

1. **Definition**:

    - This capability enables methods to be used interchangeably across various object types.

2. **Purpose**:

- The primary purpose of polymorphism is to enhance flexibility and interoperability in code. By allowing the same method name to be used for different types of objects, polymorphism makes it easier to write generalized code that can work with any object that conforms to a specific interface.

3. **Benefits:**
    - **Code Reusability:** Polymorphism allows for writing more generic and reusable code that can operate on different data types.
    - **Simplified Code:** Reduces the complexity of the code by allowing a single interface to interact with different object types.
    - **Increased Flexibility:** Makes it easier to add new classes or methods without changing existing code.

Benefits of OOP

Modularity in Object-Oriented Programming (OOP)

1. **Definition:**
    - Modularity refers to the design principle of breaking down a complex system into smaller, self-contained components or modules. In OOP, these modules are typically represented by classes and objects, which encapsulate both data and behavior.

2. **Purpose:**
    - The main goal of modularity is to enhance code organization and manageability. By dividing a large program into smaller, manageable parts, developers can focus on individual components without getting overwhelmed by the overall

complexity.

3. **Example**: Here's a simple example in Python demonstrating modularity through classes:

```
python
class Car:
def __init__(self, make, model):
self.make = make
self.model = model
def start_engine(self):
return f"{self.make} {self.model} engine started."
class Garage:
def __init__(self):
self.cars = [ ]
def add_car(self, car: Car):
self.cars.append(car)
return f"{car.make} {car.model} added to garage."
def list_cars(self):
return [f"{car.make} {car.model}" for car in self.cars]
# Creating instances of Car
car1 = Car("Toyota", "Corolla")
car2 = Car("Honda", "Civic")
# Using the Garage class to manage cars
garage = Garage()
print(garage.add_car(car1)) # Output: Toyota Corolla added to garage.
print(garage.add_car(car2)) # Output: Honda Civic added to garage.
print(garage.list_cars()) # Output: ['Toyota Corolla', 'Honda Civic']
```

4. **Key Points in the Example:**

- The Car class represents individual car objects with specific attributes and behaviors.
- The Garage class manages a collection of Car objects, demonstrating how modules can interact.
- Each class has a clear purpose, making the code organized and easier to maintain.

Reusability in Object-Oriented Programming (OOP)

1. **Definition**:

    - This is primarily achieved through concepts like inheritance, composition, and the use of libraries.

2. **Purpose**:

    - The main goal of reusability is to save time and resources by allowing developers to leverage previously written and tested code. This leads to increased productivity and consistency across applications.

3. **Mechanisms for Reusability**:

    - **Inheritance**:

        - This promotes a hierarchical structure where common behavior is defined in a base class.

    - **Composition**:

        - Instead of relying solely on inheritance, classes can be composed of other classes. This allows for flexible combinations of functionalities and promotes code reuse without creating rigid hierarchies.

- **Libraries and Frameworks**:
    - Pre-written libraries and frameworks provide reusable components that can be integrated into new applications. These resources encapsulate common functionalities, enabling developers to focus on the unique aspects of their projects.

4. **Benefits**:
    - **Reduced Development Time**: Reusing code minimizes the effort required to build new features or applications.
    - **Consistency**: Reusing established code helps maintain consistent behavior and standards across different parts of an application or across multiple projects.
    - **Easier Maintenance**: When code is reused, any updates or bug fixes need to be made only once, rather than in multiple places, making maintenance more efficient.

5. **Example**: Here's a Python example demonstrating reusability through inheritance:

```
python
class Vehicle: # Base class
def __init__(self, make, model):
self.make = make
self.model = model
def display_info(self):
return f"{self.make} {self.model}"
class Car(Vehicle): # Subclass inheriting from Vehicle
def __init__(self, make, model, doors):
super().__init__(make, model)
self.doors = doors
def display_info(self):
return f"{super().display_info()} with {self.doors} doors"
```

class Motorcycle(Vehicle): # Another subclass inheriting from Vehicle
def display_info(self):
return f"{super().display_info()} (Motorcycle)"
# Creating instances
car = Car("Toyota", "Camry", 4)
motorcycle = Motorcycle("Harley-Davidson", "Street 750")
# Using the display_info method
print(car.display_info()) # Output: Toyota Camry with 4 doors
print(motorcycle.display_info()) # Output: Harley-Davidson Street 750 (Motorcycle)

6. **Key Points in the Example:**

    - The Vehicle class serves as a reusable base class with common attributes and methods.
    - The Car and Motorcycle classes inherit from Vehicle, reusing its functionality while adding specific behaviors.
    - This structure allows for easy extension and modification without rewriting shared code.

- **Maintainability:**

1. **Definition:**

    - Maintainability in OOP refers to the ease with which a software system can be updated, modified, or extended over time. OOP's structure allows classes and objects to be altered independently, reducing the impact of changes on the overall system.

2. **Purpose:**

    - The primary goal of maintainability is to facilitate ongoing development and adaptation of software to meet new requirements or fix issues without extensive rework. This is crucial for long-term project sustainability.

3. **Key Aspects of Maintainability**:

   - **Encapsulation**: By bundling data and methods within classes, OOP restricts direct access to an object's internal state. This allows for changes to the implementation without affecting external code that interacts with the object.
   - **Modularity**: Breaking down a system into smaller, self-contained modules (classes) enables developers to focus on individual parts. This modular structure makes it easier to understand and update specific components without risking unintended side effects in others.
   - **Inheritance**: Inheritance allows subclasses to inherit functionality from superclasses while being free to implement their specific behaviors. This means that changes to the superclass can be propagated to subclasses, reducing redundancy and easing updates.
   - **Polymorphism**: With polymorphism, methods can be used interchangeably across different classes. This flexibility allows for easier integration of new functionality without disrupting existing code.

4. **Benefits**:

   - **Faster Updates**: Developers can implement changes or add features more quickly because modifications are localized to specific classes or modules.
   - **Reduced Errors**: Isolated changes minimize the risk of introducing bugs into unrelated parts of the system, enhancing overall code reliability.
   - **Easier Debugging**: When issues arise, maintainability allows for targeted troubleshooting within individual modules, making it simpler to identify and resolve problems.

5. **Key Points in the Example:**

   - The User class is easy to modify; adding a new attribute (email) did not require changes to the Admin class.
   - Each class maintains its own functionality, ensuring that changes in one do not adversely affect others. independently without affecting the entire system.

- **Flexibility and Scalability:**

OOP allows for more dynamic and adaptable systems. New features can be added w Flexibility and Scalability in Object-Oriented Programming (OOP)

1. **Definition:**

   - Flexibility in object-oriented programming (OOP) denotes a system's capacity to adjust to modifications and emerging requirements with ease. Scalability, on the other hand, pertains to a system's ability to expand and manage heightened demands or more intricate functionalities without necessitating substantial revisions.

2. **Purpose:**

   - The main purpose of flexibility and scalability in OOP is to create systems that can evolve over time, allowing developers to add new features or handle more complex operations without disrupting existing functionality. This is crucial for meeting changing user needs and scaling applications as usage increases.

3. **Key Features Supporting Flexibility and Scalability:**

- **Encapsulation**: By hiding the internal workings of classes, encapsulation allows developers to modify implementations without affecting the outside code that relies on them. This reduces the risk of breaking existing functionality when changes are made.
- **Inheritance**: New classes can be created based on existing ones, enabling developers to extend functionalities without altering the original code. This allows for the addition of new features in a controlled manner.
- **Polymorphism**: The ability to use the same interface for different underlying forms (data types) enables developers to introduce new classes that can be used interchangeably with existing ones, making it easier to adapt and extend systems.
- **Modularity**: The organization of code into distinct classes or modules promotes separation of concerns. New modules can be added or existing ones modified without impacting other parts of the system.

4. **Benefits**:

- **Ease of Enhancements**: New features can be integrated with minimal changes to the existing system, facilitating rapid development cycles.
- **Handling Complexity**: As applications expand, Object-Oriented Programming (OOP) offers the necessary framework to handle escalating complexity, thereby facilitating the development, testing, and maintenance of more extensive systems.
- **Improved Collaboration**: Different teams can work on separate modules or classes simultaneously, promoting parallel development and speeding up project timelines.

CHAPTER TWO

LISTS

Structure of a Singly Linked List:
Node Definition
A standard node within a singly linked list is comprised of:
• **Value:** The data contained in the node.
• **Next:** A reference to the subsequent node in the sequence.
Example Node Structure (in pseudocode):

```
plaintext
class Node {
data
next
}
```

Basic Operations:

1. **Initialization**

    ◦ Create an empty list with a head pointer initialized to null.

2. **Insertion**

    ◦ **To initiate the process:**
    ◦ - Establish a new node.
    ◦ - Assign its next pointer to the existing head.
    ◦ - Modify the head to reference the newly created node.

To conclude:

- Navigate through the list to identify the final node.
- Assign the next pointer of the last node to the newly created node.
- For insertion at a designated position:
- Traverse the list to the desired position.
- Update the pointers to insert the new node.

1. **Deletion**
    - **From the Beginning**:
        - Modify the head pointer to reference the second node.
    - **From the End**:
        - Traverse to the second-to-last node and set its next pointer to null.
    - **From a Specific Position**:
        - Traverse to the node before the one to be deleted.
        - Update the pointers to bypass the target node.
2. **Traversal**
    - Start from the head and follow the next pointers until reaching null, allowing access to each element.
3. **Search**
    - Traverse the list, comparing each node's data with the target value until found or reaching the end.
4. **Size Calculation**:

Maintain a counter that increases with each insertion and decreases with each deletion, or alternatively, traverse the list to tally the nodes.

7. **Verify for an Empty List: A list is considered empty when the head pointer is null.**

Advantages

- **Dynamic Size**: Can grow and shrink in size as needed.
- **Efficient Insertions/Deletions**: Insertion and deletion operations at the head exhibit a time complexity of O(1).

Disadvantages:

- **Memory Overhead**: Requires extra memory for pointers.
- **Sequential Access**: Must traverse the list to access elements, leading to O(n) time complexity for accessing elements by index.

Use Cases:

- Implementing stacks, queues, or other list-based data structures.
- Handling dynamic collections of data where the size is not known in advance.

A circularly linked list represents a modification of a standard linked list in which the final node connects back to the initial node, thereby creating a circular formation. This configuration facilitates uninterrupted navigation through the list, eliminating the possibility of encountering a null pointer at the termination. Below is a summary of circularly linked lists:

Structure of a Circularly Linked List :

Node Definition

In a manner akin to a singly linked list, each node comprises:

• Data: The value held within the node.

• Next: A reference to the subsequent node.

Example Node Structure (in pseudocode):

```
class Node {
data
next
}
```

Types of Circular Linked Lists:

1. Singly Circular Linked List: In this structure, each node directs to the subsequent node, and the final node connects back to the initial node.

2. Doubly Circular Linked List: This variant features nodes that possess pointers to both the next and the preceding nodes, with the last node linking back to the first node and vice versa.

Basic Operations:

1. **Initialization**

    ◦ Create an empty list with a head pointer initialized to null.

2. **Insertion**

At the Beginning:

- Initiate a new node.

- If the list is devoid of elements, configure its next pointer to reference itself.

- If the list contains elements, assign the new node's next pointer to the existing head, then locate the last node to adjust its next pointer to the new node, thereby establishing it as the new head.

At the End:

- This process is akin to the beginning; however, the new node is inserted subsequent to the current last node, with its next pointer updated to direct to the head.

At a Specific Position:

- Navigate through the list to reach the specified position and modify the pointers as necessary.

3. **Deletion**

From the Beginning:

- Modify the head pointer to reference the subsequent node and alter the next pointer of the last node to direct it towards the new head.

From the End:

- Navigate through the list to identify the second-to-last node and update its next pointer to link to the head.

From a Specific Position:

- This process resembles that of singly linked lists, with the added requirement of preserving the circular structure.

4. **Traversal**

   ◦ Start from the head and follow the next pointers, stopping when you reach the head again.

5. **Search**

   ◦ Traverse the list, comparing each node's data with the target value until found or returning to the head.

6. **Size Calculation**

   ◦ Maintain a counter during insertions and deletions, or traverse the list until returning to the head.

7. **Check for Empty List:**

The list is considered empty when the head pointer is null.

Example Implementation (in Python)

A straightforward implementation of a singly circular linked list in Python is presented below:

```python
class Node:
def __init__(self, data):
self.data = data
self.next = None
class CircularLinkedList:
def __init__(self):
self.head = None
def insert_at_beginning(self, data):
new_node = Node(data)
if not self.head:
self.head = new_node
new_node.next = self.head
else:
new_node.next = self.head
last_node = self.head
while last_node.next != self.head:
last_node = last_node.next
last_node.next = new_node
self.head = new_node
def insert_at_end(self, data):
new_node = Node(data)
if not self.head:
self.head = new_node
new_node.next = self.head
else:
last_node = self.head
while last_node.next != self.head:
last_node = last_node.next
last_node.next = new_node
new_node.next = self.head
def delete_node(self, key):
if not self.head:
```

```
return
current_node = self.head
if current_node.data == key:
if current_node.next == self.head: # Only one node
self.head = None
else:
last_node = self.head
while last_node.next != self.head:
last_node = last_node.next
last_node.next = current_node.next
self.head = current_node.next
return
prev_node = None
while current_node and current_node.data != key:
prev_node = current_node
current_node = current_node.next
if current_node == self.head:
return # Key not found
if current_node == self.head: # Node to delete was not found
return
prev_node.next = current_node.next
def search(self, key):
if not self.head:
return False
current_node = self.head
while True:
if current_node.data == key:
return True
current_node = current_node.next
if current_node == self.head:
break
return False
def show(self):
if self.head is None:
print("The list is empty.")
```

```
return
current_node = self.head
while True:
print(current_node.data, end=' -> ')
current_node = current_node.next
if current_node == self.head:
break
print('(head)')
# Example usage:
cll = CircularLinkedList()
cll.insert_at_end(1)
cll.insert_at_end(2)
cll.insert_at_end(3)
cll.show() # Outputs: 1 -> 2 -> 3 -> (head)
```

Advantages

- **No Null Pointers**: Allows for continuous traversal without running into null pointers.
- **Efficient Circular Traversal**: Useful for applications like round-robin scheduling.

Disadvantages

- **Complexity**: More complex to implement compared to standard linked lists.
- **Potential for Infinite Loops**: Care must be taken during traversal to avoid infinite loops.

Use Cases

- Implementing data structures for buffering (e.g., circular queues).
- Round-robin scheduling algorithms.
- Applications where circular traversal is required.

Structure of a Doubly Linked List:

Node Definition

A typical node in a doubly linked list comprises the following components:

• Value: The data held within the node.

• Next: A reference to the subsequent node in the sequence.

• Prev: A reference to the preceding node in the sequence.

Example Node Framework (in pseudocode):

```
class Node {
value
nextNode
previousNode
}
```

Basic Operations:

1. **Initialization**

Create an empty list by initializing the head pointer to null and incorporating a tail pointer to allow easy access to the end of the list.

2. **Insertion :**

At the Beginning:

- Generate a new node.
- Assign its next pointer to the existing head.
- If the list contains elements, modify the current head's previous pointer to reference the new node.
- Adjust the head pointer to point to the new node.

At the End:

- Generate a new node.
- Modify the current tail's next pointer to link to the new node.

- Set the new node's previous pointer to the current tail and update the tail pointer to reference the new node.

At a Specific Position:

- Navigate through the list to reach the specified position and adjust the pointers as necessary.

3. **Deletion**

    - **From the Beginning**:

        - Update the head pointer to the next node and set the new head's prev pointer to null.

    - **From the End**:

        - Update the tail pointer to the previous node and set the new tail's next pointer to null.

    - **From a Specific Position**:

        - Traverse to the node to be deleted and update the pointers of the adjacent nodes to bypass the target node.

4. **Traversal**

    - Start from the head and follow the next pointers to traverse forward.
    - Start from the tail and follow the prev pointers to traverse backward.

5. **Search**

   - Traverse the list in either direction, comparing each node's data with the target value until found or reaching the end.

6. **Size Calculation:**

   Keep a tally of the number of nodes during insertions and deletions, or alternatively, navigate through the list to determine the total count of nodes.

7. **Check for Empty List:**

   The list is considered empty when the head pointer is null.

Advantages:

- **Bidirectional Traversal:** Can be traversed in both forward and backward directions.
- **Easier Deletions:** No need to keep track of the previous node when deleting a node.

Disadvantages:

- **Memory Overhead:** Requires more memory for the additional pointer.
- **Complexity:** More complex to implement than singly linked lists.

Use Cases:

- Implementing complex data structures like deques and some types of caches.
- Applications requiring frequent insertion and deletion of nodes, especially at both ends.
- Scenarios needing easy backward traversal, such as undo functionality in applications.

Data structures, including singly linked lists, doubly linked lists, and arrays, exhibit a high degree of flexibility and are widely utilized across various applications in computer science and software development. The following are several common applications of lists:

1. Dynamic Arrays:

- **Use Case**: Resizing arrays in languages like Python (e.g., lists in Python).
- **Application**: Storing a collection of items where the number of elements can change dynamically, such as in managing a list of users or products.

2. Stacks:

- **Use Case**: Implemented using arrays or linked lists.
- **Application**: Employed in the administration of function calls (call stack), application undo functionalities, and depth-first search algorithms..

3. Queues:

- **Use Case**: Implemented using arrays or linked lists.
- **Application**: Used in scheduling tasks (e.g., print jobs), breadth-first search algorithms, and managing asynchronous data (like event handling).

4. Graphs:

- **Use Case**: Adjacency lists can be implemented using linked lists.
- **Application**: Representing relationships in social networks, routing algorithms in networking, and various search algorithms.

5. Hash Tables

- **Use Case**: Collision resolution can be handled using linked lists (chaining).
- **Application**: Storing key-value pairs efficiently, such as in databases or caching mechanisms.

6. Polynomials

- **Use Case**: Representing polynomials using linked lists where each node represents a term.
- **Application**: Efficient polynomial addition, subtraction, and multiplication in mathematical computations.

7. Memory Management

- **Use Case**: Free lists implemented using linked lists to manage available memory blocks.
- **Application**: Dynamic memory allocation in operating systems.

8. Text Editors

- **Use Case**: Implementing features like undo/redo using stacks or managing lines of text using linked lists.
- **Application**: Efficient text manipulation and navigation in text editors.

9. Music Playlists

- **Use Case**: Representing a playlist where songs can be added, removed, or reordered.
- **Application**: Streaming services and media players use lists to manage and display playlists.

10. Event Handling

- **Use Case**: Managing a list of events or tasks in event-driven programming.
- **Application**: GUI applications where user actions (like clicks) are queued for processing.

11. Game Development

- **Use Case**: Managing lists of game entities (players, enemies, items).
- **Application**: Efficiently adding or removing entities during gameplay and keeping track of active entities.

12. Graphs and Trees

- **Use Case**: Traversing tree structures using lists to hold nodes at each level.
- **Application**: Representing file systems, hierarchical data, and organizational structures.

13. Simulation

- **Use Case**: Managing entities in simulations (e.g., particles in physics simulations).
- **Application**: Simulating real-world scenarios where elements need to be added or removed dynamically.

14. Caching

- **Use Case**: Implementing cache mechanisms using lists to track recently used items (e.g., LRU cache).
- **Application**: Improving performance by storing frequently accessed data in memory.

The Stack Abstract Data Type (ADT) represents a collection that adheres to the Last In, First Out (LIFO) principle, indicating that the most recently added item is the first to be removed. Stacks are frequently utilized in programming for purposes such as managing function calls, implementing undo features, and various other applications. Below is a comprehensive overview of the Stack ADT.

Key Operations

1. **Push**: Insert an item at the top of the stack.
   - **Operation**: push(item)
   - **Time Complexity**: O(1)
2. **Pop**: Eliminate and retrieve the uppermost element from the stack.
   - **Operation**: pop()
   - **Time Complexity**: O(1)
   - **Error Handling**: If the stack is devoid of elements, an error indicating underflow is triggered.
3. **Peek (or Top)**: Return the top element without removing it.
   - **Operation**: peek()
   - **Time Complexity**: O(1)
   - **Error Handling**: If the stack is empty, an error is raised.
4. **isEmpty**: Check if the stack is empty.
   - **Operation**: isEmpty()
   - **Time Complexity**: O(1)
5. **Size**: Provide the count of elements present in the stack.
   - **Operation**: size()
   - **Time Complexity**: O(1)

Implementations

Stacks can be implemented using various data structures, including:

1. **Array-Based Implementation**

    - **Fixed Size**: The stack has a maximum size defined at initialization.
    - **Dynamic Size**: The stack resizes as needed (e.g., using dynamic arrays).
    - **Example**:

```
Python
class Stack:
def __init__(self):
self.items = []
def push(self, item):
self.items.append(item)
def pop(self):
if self.is_empty():
raise IndexError("Cannot pop from an empty stack")
return self.items.pop()
def peek(self):
if self.is_empty():
raise IndexError("Cannot peek from an empty stack")
return self.items[-1]
def is_empty(self):
return len(self.items) == 0
def size(self):
return len(self.items)
```

2. **Implementation Based on Linked Lists.**

Each node represents an element in the stack, with a pointer to the next node.

Allows for dynamic sizing without a predefined limit.

- **Example**:

Python

```
class Node:
def __init__(self, value):
self.value = value
self.next_node = None
class Stack:
def __init__(self):
self.top_node = None
self.size_count = 0
def push(self, value):
new_node = Node(value)
new_node.next_node = self.top_node
self.top_node = new_node
self.size_count += 1
def pop(self):
if self.is_empty():
raise IndexError("Cannot pop from an empty stack")
value = self.top_node.value
self.top_node = self.top_node.next_node
self.size_count -= 1
return value
def peek(self):
if self.is_empty():
raise IndexError("Cannot peek from an empty stack")
return self.top_node.value
def is_empty(self):
return self.top_node is None
def size(self):
return self.size_count
```

Applications

- **Function Call Management**: Stacks are used to manage function calls in programming languages (call stack).
- **Backtracking Algorithms**: Used in algorithms like depth-first search and puzzles (e.g., mazes, N-Queens).
- **Expression Evaluation**: Used to evaluate expressions and convert between infix, prefix, and postfix notations.
- **Undo Mechanisms**: Used in applications like text editors to store previous states.
- **Syntax Parsing**: Used in compilers to check for balanced parentheses and other syntax structures.

The Queue Abstract Data Type (ADT) represents a collection that adheres to the First In, First Out (FIFO) principle, indicating that the initial item inserted into the queue is the first to be extracted. Queues find extensive application in numerous scenarios, including task scheduling, request management, and resource allocation. Below is a comprehensive examination of the Queue ADT.

Key Operations

1. Enqueue: Insert an element at the end of the queue.

- Operation: enqueue(item)
- Time Complexity: O(1)

2. Dequeue: Remove and return the element at the front of the queue.

- Operation: dequeue()
- Time Complexity: O(1)
- Error Handling: An error (underflow) is triggered if the queue is empty.

3. Front (or Peek): Retrieve the front element without removing it from the queue.

- Operation: front()
- Time Complexity: O(1)
- Error Handling: An error is raised if the queue is empty.

4. isEmpty: Determine whether the queue is empty.

- Operation: isEmpty()
- Time Complexity: O(1)

5. **Size:** Provide the count of elements present in the queue.

- Operation: size()
- Time Complexity: O(1)

Implementations:
Queues can be constructed utilizing various data structures.

1. **Array-Based Implementation**

    - **Fixed Size**: The queue has a maximum size defined at initialization.
    - **Dynamic Size**: The queue resizes as needed (e.g., using dynamic arrays).
    - **Circular Queue**: An efficient way to use array space by wrapping around.
    - **Example**:

```
Python
class Queue:
def __init__(self, max_size):
self.max_size = max_size
self.items = []
def enqueue(self, item):
if len(self.items) >= self.max_size:
raise OverflowError("Queue is at capacity")
```

```
self.items.append(item)
def dequeue(self):
if self.is_empty():
raise IndexError("Cannot dequeue from an empty queue")
return self.items.pop(0)
def front(self):
if self.is_empty():
raise IndexError("Cannot access front of an empty queue")
return self.items[0]
def is_empty(self):
return len(self.items) == 0
def size(self):
return len(self.items)
```

2. Implementation Using Linked List

- Each node in this structure signifies an element within the queue and contains pointers to the subsequent node.
- This approach facilitates dynamic sizing without the necessity for a predetermined limit.
- Example:

```python
class Node:
def __init__(self, data):
self.data = data
self.next = None
class Queue:
def __init__(self):
self.front = None
self.rear = None
self.count = 0
def enqueue(self, item):
new_node = Node(item)
if self.is_empty():
self.front = self.rear = new_node
else:
self.rear.next = new_node
```

```
self.rear = new_node
self.count += 1
def dequeue(self):
if self.is_empty():
raise IndexError("Dequeue from empty queue")
item = self.front.data
self.front = self.front.next
self.count -= 1
if self.is_empty(): # If the queue becomes empty
self.rear = None
return item
def front(self):
if self.is_empty():
raise IndexError("Front from empty queue")
return self.front.data
def is_empty(self):
return self.front is None
def size(self):
return self.count
```

Applications

- **Task Scheduling**: The organization of tasks within operating systems, specifically concerning the scheduling of processes.
- **Breadth-First Search (BFS):** A technique employed in graph algorithms to systematically investigate nodes in a level-wise manner.
- **Print Spooling**: Managing print jobs in a queue until they are printed.
- **Call Center Management**: Handling customer service calls in the order they are received.
- **Data Buffers**: Temporary storage for data packets in networking (e.g., buffering in streaming).

A Double-Ended Queue (Deque) is a type of data structure that facilitates the insertion and removal of elements from both ends. This capability enables elements to be added or deleted from either the front or the back, thereby providing greater flexibility compared to traditional queues, which restrict operations to a single end.

Key Operations

1. Insert at Front: Place an element at the beginning of the deque.

- Operation: add_front(item)
- Time Complexity: O(1)

2. Insert at Rear: Place an element at the end of the deque.

- Operation: add_rear(item)
- Time Complexity: O(1)

3. **Remove from Front:** Eliminate and return the element located at the front of the deque.

- Operation: remove_front()
- Time Complexity: O(1)
- Error Handling: An error (underflow) is triggered if the deque is empty.

4.Remove from Rear: Remove and return the rear element of the deque.

   - **Operation**: remove_rear()
   - **Time Complexity**: O(1)
   - **Error Handling**: If the deque is empty, an error is raised.

2. **Peek Front**: Return the front element without removing it.

- **Operation**: peek_front()
- **Time Complexity**: O(1)
- **Error Handling**: If the deque is empty, an error is raised.

3. **Peek Rear**: Return the rear element without removing it.

   - **Operation**: peek_rear()
   - **Time Complexity**: O(1)
   - **Error Handling**: If the deque is empty, an error is raised.

4. **isEmpty**: Check if the deque is empty.

   - **Operation**: is_empty()
   - **Time Complexity**: O(1)

5. **Size**: Return the number of elements in the deque.

   - **Operation**: size()
   - **Time Complexity**: O(1)

Implementations

Deques can be implemented using various data structures:

1. **Array-Based Implementation**

   - A circular array can be used to efficiently manage the front and rear pointers.
   - **Example**:

```python
class Deque:
def __init__(self, max_size):
self.max_size = max_size
self.items = [None] * max_size
self.front = -1
```

```
self.rear = -1
def add_to_front(self, item):
if self.is_full():
raise OverflowError("Deque is full")
if self.is_empty():
self.front = self.rear = 0
else:
self.front = (self.front - 1) % self.max_size
self.items[self.front] = item
def add_to_rear(self, item):
if self.is_full():
raise OverflowError("Deque is full")
if self.is_empty():
self.front = self.rear = 0
else:
self.rear = (self.rear + 1) % self.max_size
self.items[self.rear] = item
def remove_from_front(self):
if self.is_empty():
raise IndexError("Remove from empty deque")
item = self.items[self.front]
if self.front == self.rear: # Only one element
self.front = self.rear = -1
else:
self.front = (self.front + 1) % self.max_size
return item
def remove_from_rear(self):
if self.is_empty():
raise IndexError("Remove from empty deque")
item = self.items[self.rear]
if self.front == self.rear: # Only one element
self.front = self.rear = -1
else:
self.rear = (self.rear - 1) % self.max_size
return item
```

```
def peek_at_front(self):
if self.is_empty():
raise IndexError("Peek from empty deque")
return self.items[self.front]
def peek_at_rear(self):
if self.is_empty():
raise IndexError("Peek from empty deque")
return self.items[self.rear]
```

```
def is_empty(self):
return self.front == -1
def is_full(self):
return (self.rear + 1) % self.max_size == self.front
def size(self):
if self.is_empty():
return 0
return (self.rear - self.front + 1) % self.max_size
```

1. **Linked List-Based Implementation:**

Each node contains a pointer to the next and previous nodes, allowing for dynamic sizing.

- **Example:**

```
class Node:
def __init__(self, data):
self.data = data
self.prev = None
self.next = None
class Deque:
def __init__(self):
self.front = None
self.rear = None
self.count = 0
```

```
def add_front(self, item):
new_node = Node(item)
if self.is_empty():
self.front = self.rear = new_node
else:
new_node.next = self.front
self.front.prev = new_node
self.front = new_node
self.count += 1
def add_rear(self, item):
new_node = Node(item)
if self.is_empty():
self.front = self.rear = new_node
else:
new_node.prev = self.rear
self.rear.next = new_node
self.rear = new_node
self.count += 1
def remove_front(self):
if self.is_empty():
raise IndexError("Cannot remove from an empty deque")
item = self.front.data
self.front = self.front.next
if self.front: # Adjust the previous pointer
self.front.prev = None
else: # The deque is now empty
self.rear = None
self.count -= 1
return item
def remove_rear(self):
if self.is_empty():
raise IndexError("Remove from empty deque")
item = self.rear.data
self.rear = self.rear.prev
if self.rear: # Update the next pointer
```

```
self.rear.next = None
else: # Deque became empty
self.front = None
self.count -= 1
return item
def peek_front(self):
if self.is_empty():
raise IndexError("Cannot peek from an empty deque")
return self.front.data
def peek_rear(self):
if self.is_empty():
raise IndexError("Cannot peek from an empty deque")
return self.rear.data
def is_empty(self):
return self.front is None
def size(self):
return self.count
```

Applications

- **Task Scheduling**: Useful in scenarios where tasks need to be processed from both ends (e.g., print jobs, task prioritization).
- **Palindrome Checking**: This method can be employed to determine whether a string of characters is a palindrome by examining the characters from both ends.
- **Sliding Window Algorithms**: Efficiently managing elements in algorithms that require maintaining a window of elements (e.g., maximum/minimum in a sliding window).
- **Game Development**: Managing game states or levels, allowing easy access to the current state and previous or next states.
- **Data Buffering**: Useful in streaming applications where data can be consumed from either end.

CHAPTER THREE

SORTING AND SEARCHING

Bubble Sort is a straightforward sorting algorithm that iteratively traverses the list, comparing adjacent items and exchanging them if they are not in the correct order. This process continues until the entire list is sorted. The name "bubble sort" derives from the way smaller elements rise to the top (or front) of the list, resembling bubbles.

Characteristics

Time Complexity:

- - **Worst-case:** $O(n^2)$
- - **Average-case:** $O(n^2)$
- - **Best-case:** O(n) (applicable when the list is pre-sorted)
- - **Space Complexity:** O(1) (performs sorting in place)
- - **Stability:** Bubble sort is classified as a stable sorting algorithm, which ensures that the relative order of identical elements remains unchanged.
- - **Adaptability:** The algorithm can terminate early if the array is already sorted. .

Algorithm Steps:

1. **Initiate:** Commence with the first item in the list.
2. **Evaluate:** Assess the current item against the subsequent item.

3. Exchange: If the current item exceeds the next item, perform an exchange.

4. Proceed: Transition to the next item and reiterate the evaluation and exchange process.

5. **Continue:** Persist with this procedure for every item in the list. Following each full traversal of the list, the largest unsorted item will be positioned correctly.

6. **Conclude:** Repeat the aforementioned steps until a complete traversal occurs without any exchanges, signifying that the list is fully sorted.

Example Code (in Python):

Here is an alternative implementation of the Bubble Sort algorithm in Python:

```python
def bubble_sort(array):
length = len(array)
for i in range(length):
is_swapped = False
for j in range(0, length - i - 1): # The last i elements are already sorted
if array[j] > array[j + 1]: # Compare and swap if necessary
array[j], array[j + 1] = array[j + 1], array[j]
is_swapped = True
if not is_swapped: # If no elements were swapped, the array is sorted
break
# Example usage
array = [64, 34, 25, 12, 22, 11, 90]
bubble_sort(array)
print("Sorted array is:", array)
```

Example Walkthrough:

For the array [64, 34, 25, 12, 22, 11, 90], the procedure for sorting would be as follows:

1. **First Pass:**

    - Compare 64 and 34: Swap → [34, 64, 25, 12, 22, 11, 90]
    - Compare 64 and 25: Swap → [34, 25, 64, 12, 22, 11, 90]
    - Compare 64 and 12: Swap → [34, 25, 12, 64, 22, 11, 90]
    - Compare 64 and 22: Swap → [34, 25, 12, 22, 64, 11, 90]
    - Compare 64 and 11: Swap → [34, 25, 12, 22, 11, 64, 90]
    - Compare 64 and 90: No swap → [34, 25, 12, 22, 11, 64, 90]

2. **Subsequent Passes:**

The procedure persists until the complete array is arranged in order.

Pros and Cons

Pros:

- Simple to understand and implement.
- No additional memory required (in-place sort).

Cons:

- Inefficient for large lists due to its $O(n^2)$ complexity.
- Generally not used in practice for large datasets; other algorithms (like Quick Sort or Merge Sort) are preferred.

Selection Sort:

Selection Sort is a straightforward sorting algorithm that relies on comparisons. It partitions the input list into two segments: one that is sorted and another that remains unsorted. The algorithm consistently identifies the smallest (or largest, based on the desired order) element from the unsorted segment and transfers it to the end of the sorted segment..

Characteristics

- Time Complexity:

- O Worst-case: $O(n^2)$
- O Average-case: $O(n^2)$
- O Best-case: $O(n^2)$
- Space Complexity: O(1) (sorting performed in-place)
- **Stability**: Selection sort is generally not stable, as equal elements may not maintain their original relative order.
- **Non-Adaptive**: The performance does not improve when the input is partially sorted.

Algorithm Steps

1. Initiate: Commence with the initial element in the list as the starting point for the sorted segment.

2. Identify the Minimum: Examine the unsorted portion of the list to locate the smallest element.

3. Exchange: Interchange the smallest identified element with the first element of the unsorted segment.

4. Adjust the Boundary: Shift the boundary separating the sorted and unsorted sections one element to the right.

5. Iterate: Persist with this procedure until the complete list is sorted.

Here is an alternative version of the provided text:

Example Code (in Python):

Below is a straightforward implementation of the Selection Sort algorithm in Python:

```
```python
def selection_sort(arr):
n = len(arr)
for i in range(n):
# Assume the first element of the unsorted section is the minimum
min_index = i
for j in range(i + 1, n):
if arr[j] < arr[min_index]: # Identify the smallest element
min_index = j
```
```

```
    # Exchange the identified minimum element with the first element of the unsorted section
    arr[i], arr[min_index] = arr[min_index], arr[i]
# Example usage
arr = [64, 25, 12, 22, 11]
selection_sort(arr)
print("Sorted array is:", arr)
```

Example Walkthrough

For the array [64, 25, 12, 22, 11], the sorting process would look like this:

1. **First Pass:**
   - Find the minimum (11) in the entire array.
   - Swap 11 with 64: [11, 25, 12, 22, 64]
2. **Second Pass:**
   - Find the minimum (12) in the subarray [25, 12, 22, 64].
   - Swap 12 with 25: [11, 12, 25, 22, 64]
3. **Third Pass:**
   - Find the minimum (22) in the subarray [25, 22, 64].
   - Swap 22 with 25: [11, 12, 22, 25, 64]
4. **Fourth Pass:**
   - The minimum in the last two elements is already in order.
   - No swap needed: [11, 12, 22, 25, 64]

Pros and Cons

Pros:

- Simple and easy to implement.
- Does not require additional memory (in-place sort).

Cons:

- Inefficient on large lists due to its $O(n^2)$ complexity.
- Generally not used in practice for large datasets, as better algorithms exist (like Quick Sort or Merge Sort).

Insertion Sort:

Insertion Sort is a straightforward and easy-to-understand sorting algorithm that constructs the final sorted array incrementally, one element at a time. This process can be likened to the method of sorting playing cards in one's hands. The algorithm operates by partitioning the array into a sorted portion and an unsorted portion, continuously selecting an element from the unsorted section and placing it in its appropriate position within the sorted section.

Characteristics:

• **Time Complexity:**

o **Worst-case:** $O(n^2)$

o **Average-case:** $O(n^2)$

o **Best-case:** $O(n)$ (applicable when the array is pre-sorted)

• **Space Complexity: O(1) (utilizes in-place sorting)**

• **Stability:** Insertion sort is stable, ensuring that equal elements retain their original order.

• **Adaptability:** Exhibits improved performance when the array is partially sorted.

Algorithm Steps:

1. Initiate the process by focusing on the second element, as the first element is already sorted.

2. Choose the next element from the portion that remains unsorted.

3. Evaluate and position: Compare the chosen element with those in the sorted section, shifting any elements that exceed the

chosen element to the right.

4. Position the chosen element appropriately within the sorted section.

5. Iterate: Maintain the procedure until the complete array is arranged in order.

Example Code (in Python):

Here is an alternative version of the provided text:

Example Code (in Python):

The following is a straightforward implementation of the Insertion Sort algorithm in Python:

```python
def insertion_sort(arr):
for i in range(1, len(arr)):
key = arr[i] # The element to be inserted
j = i - 1
# Shift elements of arr[0..i-1] that are greater than key
# to one position ahead of their current location
while j >= 0 and arr[j] > key:
arr[j + 1] = arr[j]
j -= 1
arr[j + 1] = key # Place the key in its appropriate position
# Example usage
arr = [64, 25, 12, 22, 11]
insertion_sort(arr)
print("Sorted array is:", arr)
```

Example Walkthrough:

For the array [64, 25, 12, 22, 11], the sorting process would look like this:

1. **Initial State:** [64 | 25, 12, 22, 11] (the vertical bar indicates the sorted section)
2. **First Pass (Insert 25):**
    - Compare 25 with 64: Move 64 to the right.

- Insert 25: [25, 64 | 12, 22, 11]

3. **Second Pass (Insert 12):**

   - Compare 12 with 64: Move 64 to the right.
   - Compare 12 with 25: Move 25 to the right.
   - Insert 12: [12, 25, 64 | 22, 11]

4. **Third Pass (Insert 22):**

   - Compare 22 with 64: Move 64 to the right.
   - Compare 22 with 25: Move 25 to the right.
   - Insert 22: [12, 22, 25, 64 | 11]

5. **Fourth Pass (Insert 11):**

   - Compare 11 with 64: Move 64 to the right.
   - Compare 11 with 25: Move 25 to the right.
   - Compare 11 with 22: Move 22 to the right.
   - Compare 11 with 12: Move 12 to the right.
   - Insert 11: [11, 12, 22, 25, 64]

Pros and Cons:
Pros:

- Simple to implement and understand.
- Efficient for small datasets or nearly sorted arrays.
- In-place sorting requires minimal additional memory.

Cons:

- This method exhibits inefficiency with extensive lists, as it operates with a time complexity of $O(n^2)$.
- Furthermore, it is not appropriate for handling large datasets when compared to more sophisticated algorithms such as Quick

Sort or Merge Sort.

Merge Sort

Merge Sort is an efficient sorting algorithm that utilizes a comparison-based approach and adheres to the divide-and-conquer strategy. It splits the input array into two segments, sorts each segment recursively, and subsequently combines the sorted segments into a single sorted array. This algorithm is especially advantageous for handling large datasets and is recognized for its time complexity of O(n log n).

Characteristics

• Time Complexity:

o Worst-case: O(n log n)

o Average-case: O(n log n)

o Best-case: O(n log n)

• Space Complexity: O(n) (necessitates extra space for temporary arrays)

• Stability: Merge Sort is stable; it preserves the relative order of equal elements.

• Non-Adaptive: The efficiency does not enhance when the input is partially sorted.

Algorithm Steps

1. Partition: Separate the array into two equal parts.

2. Overcome: Sort each half recursively.

3. Integrate: Combine the two sorted parts into one cohesive sorted array.

Example Code (in Python)

Here's a simple implementation of Merge Sort in Python:

```
Python
def merge_sort(array):
if len(array) > 1:
midpoint = len(array) // 2 # Determine the midpoint of the array
left_part = array[:midpoint] # Split the array into two halves
right_part = array[midpoint:]
```

```
merge_sort(left_part) # Recursively sort the left half
merge_sort(right_part) # Recursively sort the right half
i = j = k = 0 # Initialize indices for left_part, right_part, and the main array
# Transfer data to temporary arrays L[] and R[]
while i < len(left_part) and j < len(right_part):
if left_part[i] < right_part[j]:
array[k] = left_part[i]
i += 1
else:
array[k] = right_part[j]
j += 1
k += 1
# Check for any remaining elements
while i < len(left_part):
array[k] = left_part[i]
i += 1
k += 1
while j < len(right_part):
array[k] = right_part[j]
j += 1
k += 1
# Example usage
array = [64, 25, 12, 22, 11]
merge_sort(array)
print("Sorted array is:", array)
```

Example Walkthrough

For the array [64, 25, 12, 22, 11], the sorting process would look like this:

1. **Divide**: Split the array into two halves.
   - [64, 25, 12] and [22, 11]
2. **Further Divide**:

    - [64] and [25, 12]
    - [25] and [12]
    - [22] and [11]

3. **Conquer** (Sort):

    - Merge [25] and [12] to get [12, 25]
    - Merge [64] with [12, 25] to get [12, 25, 64]
    - Merge [22] and [11] to get [11, 22]

4. **Combine** (Final Merge):

    - Merge [12, 25, 64] and [11, 22]:

        - Result: [11, 12, 22, 25, 64]

Pros and Cons

Pros:

- This algorithm demonstrates efficiency with large datasets, maintaining a time complexity of O(n log n).
- It is a stable sorting method and performs effectively with linked lists as well as in external sorting scenarios.

Cons:

- This approach necessitates extra memory for temporary arrays, resulting in a space complexity of O(n).
- Additionally, it is not as efficient as alternative algorithms such as Quick Sort when applied to smaller datasets in practical scenarios.

Quick Sort

Quick Sort is an efficient and commonly utilized sorting algorithm that employs a divide-and-conquer approach. The algorithm operates by choosing a "pivot" element from the array and dividing the remaining elements into two sub-arrays based on their comparison to the pivot, categorizing them as either less than or greater than the pivot. Subsequently, the sub-arrays are sorted through a recursive process.

- **Characteristics :**
- Time Complexity:

o Worst-case: $O(n^2)$ (occurs when the smallest or largest element is repeatedly selected as the pivot)

o Average-case: O(n log n)

o Best-case: O(n log n) (happens when the pivot evenly splits the array into two halves)

- Space Complexity: O(log n) for the recursive stack in the best-case scenario and O(n) in the worst-case scenario.
- Stability: Quick Sort is not a stable sorting algorithm; equal elements may not retain their original order.
- In-Place: It utilizes a minimal amount of additional storage space. .

Example Code (in Python)

Here is an alternative implementation of Quick Sort in Python:

Python

```
def quick_sort(arr):
if len(arr) <= 1:
return arr # Base case: arrays with 0 or 1 element are inherently
sorted
pivot = arr[-1] # Selecting the last element as the pivot
left = []
right = []
for x in arr[:-1]: # Exclude the pivot from the iteration
if x < pivot:
left.append(x)
```

```
else:
right.append(x)
# Recursively apply quick_sort and merge the results
return quick_sort(left) + [pivot] + quick_sort(right)
# Example usage
arr = [64, 25, 12, 22, 11]
sorted_arr = quick_sort(arr)
print("Sorted array is:", sorted_arr)
```

Example Walkthrough:

For the array [64, 25, 12, 22, 11], the sorting process would look like this:

1. **Choose a Pivot**: Let's choose 11 as the pivot (last element).
2. **Partitioning**:
   - Elements less than 11: []
   - Elements greater than 11: [64, 25, 12, 22]
   - Combine: [11] + [] + [64, 25, 12, 22]
3. **Recursion**:
   - Sort [64, 25, 12, 22] with 22 as the pivot:
     - Less than 22: [12]
     - Greater than 22: [64, 25]
     - Combine: [12] + [22] + [64, 25]
4. **Continue Recursion**:
   - Sort [64, 25] with 25 as the pivot:
     - Less than 25: []
     - Greater than 25: [64]
     - Combine: [25] + [64]

5. **Combine All**: Finally, combine the sorted parts:

    - [11] + [12] + [22] + [25] + [64]
    - Result: [11, 12, 22, 25, 64]

Pros and Cons

Pros:

- Typically, it demonstrates greater efficiency in practical applications compared to other O(n log n) algorithms such as Merge Sort and Heap Sort.
- Additionally, it performs in-place sorting, which minimizes memory usage.

Cons:

- The worst-case time complexity is $O(n^2)$, although this can be alleviated through effective pivot selection techniques.
- Additionally, it is important to note that this sorting algorithm is not stable.

Linear Search

Linear Search is a simple algorithm utilized to locate a particular element within a list or array. It methodically examines each element in the data structure one by one until the target element is identified or the end of the list is encountered.

Characteristics

1. Time Complexity:

- Worst-case: O(n) (occurs when the element is absent or located at the end)

- Average-case: O(n)

- Best-case: O(1) (happens when the element is the first in the list)

2. Space Complexity: O(1) (requires a fixed amount of extra space)

3. Stability: Linear Search maintains stability; it preserves the original order of elements.

4. Adaptability: This method is applicable to both sorted and unsorted datasets.

Algorithm Steps

1. **Start**: Begin at the first element of the list.
2. **Compare**: Check if the current element matches the target value.
3. **Move Forward**: If the current element does not match, move to the next element.
4. **Repeat**: Continue this process until the element is found or the end of the list is reached.
5. **Return Result**: If found, return the index of the element; if not, indicate that the element is not present.

Example Code (in Python)

Here is a straightforward implementation of Linear Search in Python:

```
Python
def linear_search(arr, target):
for index, element in enumerate(arr):
if element == target:
return index # Target found
return -1 # Target not found
# Example usage
arr = [5, 3, 8, 4, 2]
target = 4
result = linear_search(arr, target)
if result != -1:
print(f"Target found at index: {result}")
else:
print("Target not found.")
```

Example Walkthrough

For the array [5, 3, 8, 4, 2] and target value 4:

1. **Start at index 0**: Check 5 (not a match).
2. **Index 1**: Check 3 (not a match).
3. **Index 2**: Check 8 (not a match).
4. **Index 3**: Check 4 (match found).
5. **Return index 3**.

Pros and Cons

Pros:

- Simple and easy to implement.
- Works on both sorted and unsorted data.
- No additional memory required.

Cons:

Ineffective for handling large datasets when compared to more sophisticated search algorithms, such as Binary Search, which necessitates sorted data.

Binary Search

Binary Search is an effective algorithm utilized for locating a particular element within a sorted array or list. The method operates by continuously halving the search interval, which greatly diminishes the number of comparisons required to identify the desired value.

Characteristics :

• **Time Complexity:**

o Worst-case: O(log n)

o Average-case: O(log n)

o Best-case: O(1) (when the target element is located at the midpoint)

• **Space Complexity**: O(1) for the iterative method; O(log n) for the recursive method (attributable to the call stack).

• **Stability:** Binary Search is classified as unstable, as it does not preserve the sequence of identical elements.

• **Precondition:** The dataset must be sorted before executing a binary search.

Algorithm Steps

1. Begin by establishing two pointers: one at the start of the array (low) and the other at the end of the array (high).

2. Determine the middle index using the formula mid = (low + high) // 2.

3. **Perform a comparison:**

- If the element at the middle index matches the target, return the index.

- If the middle element is less than the target, update the low pointer to mid + 1 to search in the right half.

- If the middle element is greater than the target, update the high pointer to mid - 1 to search in the left half.

4. Continue this process until the low pointer surpasses the high pointer.

5. If the target element is not located, return -1.

Example Code (in Python):

Here's a simple implementation of Binary Search in Python:

```
def binary_search(array, target_value):
lower_bound, upper_bound = 0, len(array) - 1
while lower_bound <= upper_bound:
middle_index = (lower_bound + upper_bound) // 2
if array[middle_index] == target_value:
return middle_index # Element located
elif array[middle_index] < target_value:
lower_bound = middle_index + 1 # Continue search in the right segment
else:
upper_bound = middle_index - 1 # Continue search in the left segment
return -1 # Element not located
# Example of usage
array = [1, 2, 4, 5, 7, 8, 9] # The array must be sorted
target_value = 5
result_index = binary_search(array, target_value)
if result_index != -1:
```

```
print(f"Element found at index: {result_index}")
else:
print("Element not found.")
```

Example Walkthrough

For the sorted array [1, 2, 4, 5, 7, 8, 9] and target value 5:

1. **Initial State:** low = 0, high = 6
2. **First Mid Calculation:**
    - mid = (0 + 6) // 2 = 3 (value is 5)
    - Target found at index 3.

Pros and Cons

Pros:

- Much faster than linear search for large datasets due to O(log n) time complexity.
- Efficient use of comparisons reduces the number of elements to be searched.

Cons:

- Requires the data to be sorted beforehand.
- More complex to implement than linear search.

CHAPTER FOUR

HASHING

Hashing

Hashing is a method employed to transform input data, which often varies in length, into a fixed-size output, usually referred to as a hash code or hash value. This technique is frequently utilized in data structures like hash tables, facilitating efficient data retrieval, storage, and management.

Key Concepts

1. Hash Function: A hash function is a computational process that takes an input, referred to as a "key," and generates a fixed-length sequence of bytes. The resulting output, known as a hash code or hash value, is ideally unique for each distinct input. High-quality hash functions are engineered to reduce the likelihood of collisions, which occur when two different inputs yield the same hash value.

2. Collision: A collision is defined as the scenario in which two separate inputs result in the same hash value. Robust hash functions aim to minimize the occurrence of such collisions.

3. Hash Table: A hash table is a specialized data structure that employs hashing techniques to organize key-value pairs. It facilitates average-case constant time complexity (O(1)) for operations such as searching, inserting, and deleting entries.

How Hashing Works

1. Input Handling: Upon the insertion of a key into a hash table, the hash function evaluates it to generate a hash code.

2. Index Determination: This hash code is subsequently converted into an index for placement within the hash table, typically employing a modulus operation relative to the size of the table.

3. Data Preservation: The key-value pair is then recorded at the determined index within the hash table.

4. Value Access: To access a value, the identical hash function is utilized on the key to ascertain the index, from which the corresponding value is retrieved.

Example Code (in Python)

Here's a simple implementation of a hash table using Python's built-in dictionary, which uses hashing internally:

```
Python
class HashTable:
def __init__(self):
self.table = {}
def insert(self, key, value):
self.table[key] = value # Stores the value associated with the hashed key
def get(self, key):
return self.table.get(key, None) # Retrieves the value for the specified key, or None if absent
def delete(self, key):
if key in self.table:
del self.table[key] # Deletes the key-value pair from the table
# Example usage
hash_table = HashTable()
hash_table.insert("apple", 10)
hash_table.insert("banana", 20)
print("Value for 'apple':", hash_table.get("apple")) # Output: 10
hash_table.delete("apple")
print("Value for 'apple' after deletion:", hash_table.get("apple")) # Output: None
```

Pros and Cons

Pros:

- **Fast Lookups**: Hash tables provide average-case O(1) time complexity for search, insert, and delete operations.
- **Flexible Size**: Can dynamically resize when the load factor increases.

Cons:

- **Collisions**: Handling collisions can complicate the implementation and degrade performance if not managed properly.
- **Space Overhead**: Hash tables may require more space than the number of entries due to wasted slots and the need for resizing.
- **Unordered**: Hash tables do not maintain the order of elements, which can be a drawback for certain applications.

Applications of Hashing

1. **Data Retrieval**: Quickly accessing data in databases or caching systems.
2. **Hash Maps**: Implementing associative arrays or dictionaries.
3. **Cryptography**: Creating digital signatures and checksums.
4. **Data Integrity**: Verifying data integrity in data transmission and storage.

Hash Functions:

A hash function serves as an essential element in numerous computing applications, especially within data structures such as hash tables, cryptography, and the verification of data integrity. It processes input data, which can vary in length, and generates a fixed-size output, usually represented as a string of bytes in hexadecimal format.

Key Properties of Hash Functions

Essential Characteristics of Hash Functions

1. Deterministic: The output will consistently be the same for identical inputs.

2. Fixed Output Size: The output maintains a uniform size regardless of the input size (for instance, SHA-256 consistently yields a 256-bit hash).

3. Efficient: Hash functions must be computationally efficient when processing any input.

4. Pre-image Resistance: It should be computationally challenging to deduce the original input from a given hash value.

5. Collision Resistance: Identifying two distinct inputs that generate the same hash output should be a difficult task.

6. Avalanche Effect: A minor alteration in the input (even a single bit) should result in a markedly different hash value.

Common Hash Functions:

1. MD5 (Message Digest Algorithm 5):

- Generates a hash value of 128 bits, represented by 32 hexadecimal characters.
- Although it has been extensively utilized, it is susceptible to collision attacks and is therefore not advisable for applications requiring high security.

2. SHA-1 (Secure Hash Algorithm 1):

- Generates a hash value of 160 bits, represented by 40 hexadecimal characters.
- Previously popular, it is now recognized to have vulnerabilities that render it inappropriate for secure applications.

3. SHA-256 (Secure Hash Algorithm 256):

- A member of the SHA-2 family, it produces a hash value of 256 bits.
- It is currently regarded as secure and is commonly employed in a variety of applications, including those related to blockchain technology.

4.SHA-3:

- The latest member of the Secure Hash Algorithm family, with variable output lengths (224, 256, 384, or 512 bits).
- Uses a different internal structure than previous SHA algorithms, offering enhanced security.

5.bcrypt, scrypt, and Argon2:

- Designed for hashing passwords; incorporate a "cost factor" to slow down hash generation, making brute-force attacks more difficult.

Example Code (Hashing with SHA-256)

An illustration of utilizing Python's hashlib library to calculate a SHA-256 hash is provided below:

```
python
import hashlib
def hash_string(input_string):
# Create a new sha256 hash object
sha256_hash = hashlib.sha256()
# Update the hash object with the bytes of the string
sha256_hash.update(input_string.encode())
# Return the hexadecimal representation of the digest
return sha256_hash.hexdigest()
# Example usage
input_str = "Hello, World!"
hash_value = hash_string(input_str)
print(f"SHA-256 hash of '{input_str}': {hash_value}")
```

Applications of Hash Functions

1. **Data Integrity:** Verifying that data remains unchanged during transmission or storage (utilizing checksums and digital signatures).

2. **Cryptography:** Safeguarding sensitive information (such as passwords) and creating secure tokens.

3. **Data Structures:** Utilizing hash tables to facilitate rapid data access.

4. **Blockchain:** Maintaining the integrity of transactions and blocks within the system.

5. **Unique Identifiers:** Producing distinct keys for records in databases. .

Collision handling typically refers to the methods used in computer programming, particularly in game development and simulations, to manage interactions between objects when they collide. Here are some key concepts:

1. Collision Detection

- **Bounding Volumes**: Use simple shapes (like boxes or spheres) to quickly determine if two objects might collide.
- **Spatial Partitioning**: Techniques like quad-trees or grid systems to reduce the number of collision checks by organizing objects spatially.
- **Pixel/Vertex Collision**: More precise checks that look at the actual shapes or pixels of objects, though they are computationally more expensive.

2. Collision Response

- **Elastic Collisions**: Objects bounce off each other, conserving kinetic energy.
- **Inelastic Collisions**: Objects may stick together or deform, losing some kinetic energy.
- **Sliding and Friction**: Determine how objects move post-collision, considering friction and surfaces.

3. Continuous Collision Detection (CCD)

- A technique to prevent fast-moving objects from passing through each other by checking for potential collisions along the entire path of the movement, rather than just at discrete time intervals.

4. Physics Engines

- Many developers use established physics engines (like Unity's PhysX, Box2D, or Bullet) that handle both collision detection and response, providing more realism and simplifying development.

5. Game Design Considerations

- Balance realism and performance: Decide the level of detail required for collision detection based on gameplay needs.
- Edge Cases: Plan for scenarios where objects may behave unexpectedly, like corners or edges.

6. Debugging Collisions

- Use visual aids in development to see collision boundaries, which can help in fine-tuning and troubleshooting.

Load factors, rehashing, and efficiency are critical concepts associated with hash tables, which are frequently utilized in data structures to facilitate rapid data retrieval. Below is an explanation of each concept.

1. Load Factor

- **Definition**: The load factor of a hash table is characterized as the proportion of the number of entries stored (n) to the total number of slots available (m). This is generally represented by the formula Load Factor = n/m.
- **Significance**: A load factor that is too high can lead to increased collisions (when multiple entries hash to the same slot), which can degrade performance. A load factor that is too low can result in wasted space.

2. Rehashing

- **Definition**: Rehashing is the process of resizing a hash table and recalculating the hash positions for existing entries when the load factor exceeds a certain threshold.
- **Process**:
  1. **Determine when to rehash**: Typically occurs when the load factor exceeds a predefined limit (e.g., 0.7).
  2. **Create a new, larger hash table**: Often, the new size is a prime number or double the current size to reduce collision chances.
  3. **Reinsert entries**: All existing entries must be rehashed and inserted into the new table, which can be computationally expensive but ensures better performance.
- **Impact on Performance**: Rehashing can temporarily affect performance due to the time taken to copy and reinsert entries, but it can significantly improve efficiency in the long run by reducing collisions.

3. Efficiency

- **Time Complexity**:
  - **Average Case**: O(1) for insertions, deletions, and lookups if the load factor is maintained appropriately.
  - **Worst Case**: O(n) for all operations if many collisions occur (e.g., if the hash function is poor or load factor is too high).
- **Space Complexity**: The time complexity is O(m), with m representing the number of slots in the hash table. This situation may result in inefficiencies if the load factor is excessively low, resulting in a significant number of vacant slots.

- **Trade-offs**: Balancing the load factor is crucial—keeping it low to minimize collisions vs. keeping it high to maximize space efficiency.

CHAPTER FIVE

TREES

A Binary Tree Abstract Data Type (ADT) is a particular form of tree structure in which each node can have no more than two offspring, commonly designated as the left child and the right child. The utility of binary trees spans numerous applications, attributed to their organized structure and effectiveness in performing search and sort operations. Below is a summary of the Binary Tree ADT:

Key Elements:

1. Node: The essential component of the tree, which includes:

o **Data:** The value held within the node.

o **Left Child:** A pointer or reference to the node's left child.

o **Right Child:** A pointer or reference to the node's right child.

2. Root: The uppermost node of the tree, serving as the starting point for all operations.

3. Leaf Node: A node that does not possess any children.

4. Height of the Tree: The measurement of the longest path extending from the root to a leaf.

5. Depth of a Node: The measurement of the path length from the root to that specific node.

Operations:

The following are the standard operations that can be executed on a Binary Tree Abstract Data Type (ADT):

1. Insertion:

The process of adding a new node can vary based on the type of tree (e.g., complete binary tree, binary search tree).

2. Deletion:

The act of removing a node from the tree, which may require different approaches depending on whether the node is a leaf, has one child, or has two children.

3. Traversal:

The method of visiting all nodes in a designated sequence:

- Preorder Traversal: Visit the root first, then the left subtree, followed by the right subtree.
- Inorder Traversal: Traverse the left subtree, visit the root, and then traverse the right subtree. (This method is especially beneficial in binary search trees, as it produces a sorted sequence.)
- Postorder Traversal: Traverse the left subtree, then the right subtree, and finally visit the root.
- Level-order Traversal: Visit nodes in a level-wise manner, typically utilizing a queue.

4. Searching:

The process of locating a node with a specific value. In a binary search tree, this operation is efficient as it allows for the elimination of half of the remaining nodes based on comparisons.

5. Height/Depth Calculation:

The determination of the tree's height or the depth of a particular node.

Implementation Example (in Python)

Here's a simple implementation of a Binary Tree in Python:

Python

```
class TreeNode:
def __init__(self, value):
self.value = value
self.left_child = None
self.right_child = None
class BinaryTree:
def __init__(self, root_value):
self.root = TreeNode(root_value)
```

```
def add(self, value):
self._add_recursively(self.root, value)
def _add_recursively(self, current_node, value):
if value < current_node.value:
if current_node.left_child is None:
current_node.left_child = TreeNode(value)
else:
self._add_recursively(current_node.left_child, value)
else:
if current_node.right_child is None:
current_node.right_child = TreeNode(value)
else:
self._add_recursively(current_node.right_child, value)
def inorder_display(self, node):
if node:
self.inorder_display(node.left_child)
print(node.value, end=' ')
self.inorder_display(node.right_child)
# Example Usage
binary_tree = BinaryTree(10)
binary_tree.add(5)
binary_tree.add(15)
binary_tree.add(3)
print("Inorder Display:")
binary_tree.inorder_display(binary_tree.root) # Output: 3 5 10
15
```

Applications

1. The following are key applications of various tree structures:

- **Searching and Sorting:** Binary search trees facilitate efficient search operations and enable the retrieval of sorted data.
- **Expression Trees:** These trees are utilized in compilers for the representation of expressions.

- **Heaps**: A complete binary tree structure employed in the implementation of priority queues.
- **Huffman Coding Trees**: These trees play a crucial role in algorithms designed for data compression.

Tree traversals refer to the methods employed to systematically visit every node within a tree data structure. Various traversal techniques exist, each designed for specific objectives and resulting in distinct sequences of node access. Below is a comprehensive examination of the prevalent tree traversal methods.

1. Depth-First Traversal (DFT)

This approach explores as far down a branch as possible before backtracking. The main types of depth-first traversal are:

• Preorder Traversal:

o **Sequence:** First, access the root node, then explore the left subtree, and subsequently the right subtree.

o **Application:** Commonly employed to duplicate the tree structure or to generate prefix expressions.

```
python
def preorder(node):
if node:
print(node.data, end=' ')
preorder(node.left)
preorder(node.right)
```

2. Inorder Traversal:

- Sequence: First, explore the left subtree, then visit the root node, followed by the right subtree.
- Application: Generates a sorted list of values within a binary search tree.

```
```python
def inorder(node):
if node:
inorder(node.left)
```
```

```
print(node.data, end=' ')
inorder(node.right)
```

1. **Postorder Traversal:**

- Sequence: First, explore the left subtree, then the right subtree, and finally visit the root node.
- Application: Utilized for node deletion and evaluating postfix expressions.

```python
def postorder(node):
if node:
postorder(node.left)
postorder(node.right)
print(node.data, end=' ')
```

2. Breadth-First Traversal (BFT)

This approach examines all nodes at the current depth level prior to progressing to nodes at the subsequent depth level. The most prevalent variant is as follows:

• Level-order Traversal:

o Sequence: Access nodes in a level-by-level manner, generally employing a queue.

o Application: Effective for determining the shortest path in an unweighted tree.

Python

```
from collections import deque
def level_order_traversal(root):
if root is None:
return
queue = deque([root])
while queue:
current_node = queue.popleft()
```

```
print(current_node.data, end=' ')
if current_node.left:
queue.append(current_node.left)
if current_node.right:
queue.append(current_node.right)
```

Summary of Traversal Orders:

Traversal Type	Visit Order	Common Uses
Preorder	Root → Left → Right	Copying trees, prefix expressions
Inorder	Left → Root → Right	Sorting values in binary search trees
Postorder	Left → Right → Root	Deleting trees, evaluating postfix expressions
Level-order	Level by level	Finding shortest paths, level-based processing

Applications of Tree Traversals

- **Binary Search Trees**: Efficient searching and sorting.
- **Expression Trees**: For evaluating or converting expressions.
- **File Systems**: Navigating directories and files.
- **Network Routing**: For managing and exploring networks.

Binary Search Tree (BST) is a distinct category of binary tree that preserves a sorted arrangement of its elements, facilitating efficient operations for searching, inserting, and deleting nodes. Below is a comprehensive examination of BSTs, including their characteristics and frequently performed operations.

Key Characteristics of a Binary Search Tree :

1. Node Composition:

- Each node comprises a value, a reference to the left child, and a reference to the right child.

2. Ordering Principle:
- For every node:

- All values in the left subtree are less than the value of the node.
- All values in the right subtree exceed the value of the node.

1. **Absence of Duplicate Nodes:**

Binary Search Trees generally do not permit duplicate values. If duplicates are permitted, a method must be established (for instance, storing duplicates in a list at each node).

Basic Operations:

1. **Insertion:**

To add a new value, begin at the root and evaluate it against the current node:

- If the new value is smaller, proceed to the left child.
- If it is larger, proceed to the right child.
- Continue this procedure until a null position is located for the insertion of the new node.

```python
def insert(node, key):
if node is None:
return TreeNode(key)
if key < node.data:
node.left = insert(node.left, key)
else:
node.right = insert(node.right, key)
return node
```

```
```

2. Searching:

- Commencing at the root, the process is akin to insertion:
- Should the value of the current node correspond to the target, the node is returned.
- If the target is lesser, the search continues in the left subtree.
- If the target is greater, the search proceeds to the right subtree.

```
python
def search(node, key):
if node is None or node.data == key:
return node
if key < node.data:
return search(node.left, key)
return search(node.right, key)
```

3. Deletion:

- Three cases need to be handled:

1.Leaf Node: Simply remove the node.

2.Node with One Child: Remove the node and replace it with its child.

3. Node with Two Children: Identify the node's inorder predecessor (the maximum value in the left subtree) or successor (the minimum value in the right subtree), substitute the node's value with that of the predecessor or successor, and subsequently remove the predecessor or successor.

```
python
def delete(node, key):
if node is None:
return node
if key < node.data:
node.left = delete(node.left, key)
elif key > node.data:
```

```
node.right = delete(node.right, key)
else:
# Node with only one child or no children
if node.left is None:
return node.right
elif node.right is None:
return node.left
# Node with two children
temp = min_value_node(node.right)
node.data = temp.data
node.right = delete(node.right, temp.data)
return node
def min_value_node(node):
current = node
while current.left is not None:
current = current.left
return current
```

1. **Traversal:**

- Inorder Traversal: Produces a sequence of values arranged in sorted order.
- Preorder and Postorder traversals are also relevant.

Complexity:

- **Time Complexity**:
  - The average time complexity for search, insertion, and deletion operations is O(log n). In contrast, the worst-case scenario, which occurs when the tree becomes unbalanced, results in a time complexity of O(n).
- **Space Complexity**: O(n) for storing nodes.

Advantages of BSTs

- Efficient for searching, inserting, and deleting operations.
- Ordered structure allows for easy range queries.

Disadvantages

- Performance degrades if the tree becomes unbalanced (e.g., all nodes in a line).
- Requires additional balancing methods (like AVL or Red-Black trees) for guaranteed O(log n) operations.

Applications

- Used in databases for indexing and quick search operations.
- Implementing dynamic sets and associative arrays.
- In various: algorithms, including Huffman coding trees.

AVL trees represent a category of self-balancing binary search trees (BST) that preserve their equilibrium by employing particular rotation techniques during the processes of insertion and deletion. These trees are named after their creators, Georgy Adelson-Velsky and Evgenii Landis. AVL trees guarantee that the height disparity between the left and right subtrees of any given node, referred to as the balance factor, does not exceed 1. This characteristic of balancing contributes to the efficiency of search, insertion, and deletion operations.

Rotations:

1. Balance Factor:

The balance factor of a node is calculated as the difference between the height of its left subtree and the height of its right subtree. In the context of an AVL tree, this factor can take on values of -1, 0, or +1.

2. Height-Balanced:

An AVL tree inherently preserves a balanced height, which guarantees that operations can be executed with a time complexity of O(log n).

3. Rotations:

If the balance factor of a node falls below -1 or exceeds +1 as a result of an insertion or deletion, it is necessary to rebalance the tree through the use of rotations.

Operations

1. **Insertion:**
    - Insert as in a standard BST.
    - After insertion, update the heights and check the balance factors.
    - If the tree becomes unbalanced, perform the appropriate rotation.

```
Python
class TreeNode:
def __init__(self, value):
self.value = value
self.left_child = None
self.right_child = None
self.height = 1
def insert_node(root, value):
if root is None:
return TreeNode(value)
elif value < root.value:
root.left_child = insert_node(root.left_child, value)
else:
root.right_child = insert_node(root.right_child, value)
root.height = 1 + max(calculate_height(root.left_child), calculate_height(root.right_child))
balance_factor = calculate_balance(root)
# Left Left Case
```

```
if balance_factor > 1 and value < root.left_child.value:
return perform_right_rotation(root)
# Right Right Case
if balance_factor < -1 and value > root.right_child.value:
return perform_left_rotation(root)
# Left Right Case
if balance_factor > 1 and value > root.left_child.value:
root.left_child = perform_left_rotation(root.left_child)
return perform_right_rotation(root)
# Right Left Case
if balance_factor < -1 and value < root.right_child.value:
root.right_child = perform_right_rotation(root.right_child)
return perform_left_rotation(root)
return root
def calculate_height(node):
return node.height if node else 0
def calculate_balance(node):
return calculate_height(node.left_child) - calculate_height(node.right_child)
```

1. **Deletion**:
    - Similar to a standard BST deletion.
    - After deletion, update the heights and check balance factors.
    - Perform necessary rotations to rebalance the tree.
2. **Traversal**:
    - Inorder, Preorder, and Postorder traversals can be implemented similarly to a regular BST.

Time Complexity:

- Search: O (log n)
- Insertion: O (log n)
- Deletion: O (log n)

Applications

- **Databases:** For maintaining sorted data with efficient lookups and updates.
- **Memory Management:** AVL trees can be used in scenarios requiring dynamic memory allocation.
- **Data Compression:** Used in algorithms like Huffman coding.

Advantages

- AVL trees guarantee : The time complexity for search, insertion, and deletion operations is O(log n), attributed to their balancing characteristics.
- More rigidly balanced than some other self-balancing trees (like Red-Black trees), leading to faster lookups.

Disadvantages

- The overhead of maintaining balance can result in slower insertion and deletion compared to other trees, especially for bulk insertions.
- More complex to implement compared to simpler tree structures.

Multiway Search

Multiway search trees represent a category of tree data structures that extend the concept of binary search trees by permitting each node to possess multiple children. This enhancement can lead to increased search efficiency, especially when dealing with extensive datasets. The following is a summary of multiway search trees, encompassing their various types, characteristics, and operational procedures.

Key Properties of Multiway Search Trees

1. **Node Structure:**

- Each node can contain multiple keys (values) and multiple children. The number of keys in a node determines how many children it has. For a node with kkk keys, it has k+1k + 1k+1 children.

2. Property of Ordering:

   Keys contained within a node are organized in a sorted manner. For every node:

- All keys in the left child are less than the initial key of the node.
- All keys in the right child exceed the final key of the node.
- Keys situated between the children are arranged in relation to the keys within the node.

1. **Height-Balanced**:

   - Multiway search trees aim to remain balanced, similar to binary search trees. This helps ensure efficient operations.

Types of Multiway Search Trees
1.B-Trees:

- A self-adjusting multiway search tree that preserves sorted data while facilitating searches, sequential access, insertions, and deletions in logarithmic time complexity.
- Each node is capable of containing a variable number of keys, with limits established by the tree's order (commonly represented as t):
- Each node may contain a maximum of 2t−1 keys and a minimum of t−1 keys (with the exception of the root, which may have fewer).
- All leaf nodes are positioned at the same level, thereby maintaining a balanced height.

2. B+ Trees:

- A variant of the B-tree in which all values are located at the leaf level, while internal nodes solely retain keys to facilitate search operations.
- This configuration supports efficient range queries and ordered traversal of the data elements.

3. Ternary Search Trees:

- A specific type of trie that employs three pointers for each node, allowing for the accommodation of keys that are less than, equal to, or greater than the current key.
- Particularly advantageous for the storage and retrieval of strings, making it ideal for applications resembling dictionaries.

Operations:

1. Search:

Commencing from the root, similar to the binary search method, navigate through the tree while comparing the target key with the keys present in the current node to determine the appropriate child to pursue.

2. Insertion:

Place the key in the suitable leaf node. Should the node surpass its maximum key capacity, as split is necessary:

- The median key is elevated to the parent node.
- The node is divided into two, each holding half of the keys.
- This process may necessitate recursive splitting up to the root level.

3. Deletion:

- To remove a key, first identify its location within the relevant node.

- If the key resides in an internal node, substitute it with either its predecessor or successor, and subsequently delete that key from the leaf.
- In cases where a node contains fewer than the minimum required keys post-deletion, it may need to acquire a key from a sibling or undergo merging with a sibling.

Complexity

• Search operation: O(log n)

• Insertion operation: O(log n) (amortized, considering possible splits)

• Deletion operation: O(log n) (amortized)

Applications:

• **Databases:** Multiway search trees are extensively utilized in database indexing systems to enhance the efficiency of data retrieval and storage.

• **File Systems:** B-trees and B+ trees play a crucial role in the organization and management of files and directories.

• **Memory Management:** These structures facilitate the effective storage and retrieval of data within dynamic memory allocation systems.

Advantages

- **Reduced Height**: By allowing more than two children, multiway search trees can have a lower height compared to binary search trees, improving search times.
- **Better Disk Utilization**: B-trees, in particular, are designed to minimize disk accesses, making them ideal for storage systems.

Disadvantages

- **Complexity**: The algorithms for insertion and deletion are more complex than those for binary search trees.
- **Overhead**: More pointers and keys in each node can result in higher memory overhead.

CHAPTER SIX

GRAPHS

A Graph Abstract Data Type (ADT) is a data structure that represents a collection of interconnected nodes (or vertices) and the relationships (or edges) between them. Graphs can be used to model a wide variety of real-world problems, such as social networks, transportation systems, and more. Here's an overview of the key concepts, representations, and operations associated with graphs.

Key Concepts:

1. Vertices (Nodes): The essential components of a graph, symbolizing entities such as cities or individuals.

2. Edges (Links): The connections that exist between vertices, illustrating relationships like roads or friendships. Edges can be classified as:

- Directed: The connection has a specific direction (e.g., one-way streets).
- Undirected: The connection is mutual (e.g., two-way streets).

3. Weighted Edges: Edges that possess an associated weight or cost, such as distance or time.

4. Degree: The total number of edges linked to a vertex. In directed graphs, we differentiate between:

- In-degree: The count of incoming edges.

- Out-degree: The count of outgoing edges.

5. Path: A series of vertices that are interconnected by edges.

6. **Cycle**: A path that begins and concludes at the same vertex without traversing any edge more than once.

7. Connected Graph: A graph where a path exists between every pair of vertices.

8. Subgraph: A graph created from a selection of vertices and edges from another graph.

Representations of Graphs

There are two primary ways to represent graphs in a program:

1. Adjacency Matrix:

- This structure is represented as a two-dimensional array, where the element located at row i and column j signifies the existence (and potentially the weight) of a connection between vertices i and j.
- Space Complexity: O(V^2), with V representing the total number of vertices.
- Advantages: Provides rapid access to edge information.
- Disadvantages: Inefficient in terms of space for graphs that are sparse.

```
python
# Example of an adjacency matrix
graph = [
[0, 1, 0, 0],
[1, 0, 1, 1],
[0, 1, 0, 1],
[0, 1, 1, 0]
]
```

2. **Adjacency List:**

- This representation consists of an array of lists (or a dictionary), where each index corresponds to a vertex, and the list at that index includes the vertices that are directly connected to it.

- Space Complexity: O(V + E), where E denotes the total number of edges.
- Advantages: More efficient in terms of space for sparse graphs.
- Disadvantages: Edge lookups are comparatively slower.

```
python
# Example of an adjacency list
graph = {
0: [1],
1: [0, 2, 3],
2: [1, 3],
3: [1, 2]
}
```

Operations on Graphs:

1. **Adding a Vertex**: Insert a new vertex into the graph.
2. **Adding an Edge**: Connect two vertices by adding an edge.
3. **Removing a Vertex**: Delete a vertex and its associated edges.
4. **Removing an Edge**: Disconnect two vertices by removing the edge.
5. **Traversing the Graph**:

- Depth-First Search (DFS) is a method that delves deeply into each branch of a graph or tree structure before retracing its steps.
- In contrast, Breadth-First Search (BFS) examines all adjacent vertices of a given vertex prior to progressing to the next level of neighbors.

Traversal Algorithms:

- Depth-First Search (DFS) can be executed through either recursive methods or by utilizing a stack. It is particularly effective for applications such as identifying connected components and performing topological sorting.

- In contrast, Breadth-First Search (BFS) is carried out using a queue and is advantageous for determining the shortest path in graphs that do not have weights.

Complexity:
Space Complexity:

- Adjacency Matrix: O(V^2)
- Adjacency List: O(V + E)

Time Complexity:

- Adding a vertex: O (1)
- Adding an edge: O (1) for Adjacency List or O(V) for Adjacency Matrix
- Removing a vertex: O (V + E)
- Removing an edge: O(E) for Adjacency List or O (1) for Adjacency Matrix
- Traversal (DFS/BFS): O (V + E)

Applications

- **Social Networks**: Modeling relationships between users.
- **Routing Algorithms**: Finding optimal paths in networks.
- **Web Page Ranking**: Analyzing links between web pages (e.g., PageRank).
- **Network Flow**: Problems in logistics and transportation.

Graphs can be depicted in various formats, each possessing distinct benefits and drawbacks. The two predominant forms of representation are adjacency matrices and adjacency lists. This discussion will provide an in-depth examination of these representations, as well as a few supplementary methods.

1. Adjacency Matrix

- **Structure:** A two-dimensional array (matrix) is utilized, with rows and columns corresponding to the vertices of the graph. The entry at position (i,j) signifies the existence or non-existence (and potentially the weight) of an edge connecting vertex i to vertex j.
- **Undirected Graph:** The matrix exhibits symmetry; if an edge exists between vertices i and j, then both (i,j) and (j,i) will reflect the same value.
- **Directed Graph:** The matrix may lack symmetry; the entry (i,j) denotes an edge directed from vertex i to vertex j, while (j,i) may either be zero or contain a different value.
- **Weight Representation:** In cases where edges possess weights, the matrix entry can represent the weight rather than merely indicating 0 or 1.
- **Space Complexity:** O(V^2), where V represents the total number of vertices.

Example:

Python

The following is an adjacency matrix representing an undirected graph:

```
graph_matrix = [
[0, 1, 0, 0], # Connections from vertex 0
[1, 0, 1, 1], # Connections from vertex 1
[0, 1, 0, 1], # Connections from vertex 2
[0, 1, 1, 0] # Connections from vertex 3
]
```

2. Adjacency List

- **Structure:** An array (or list) of lists (or dictionaries) where each index corresponds to a vertex, and the list at that index contains all adjacent vertices.
- **Undirected Graph:** If there's an edge between vertices iii and jjj, both iii will include jjj in its list, and jjj will include iii.

- **Directed Graph**: Only the list of the source vertex will contain the destination vertex.
- **Weight Representation**: If edges have weights, the list can store tuples of (neighbor, weight).
- **Space Complexity**: The time complexity is expressed as O(V + E), where E represents the number of edges.

Example:

python

```
# Adjacency list for an undirected graph
graph_list = {
0: [1],
1: [0, 2, 3],
2: [1, 3],
3: [1, 2]
}
```

3. Edge List

1. Structure: The representation consists of a list of edges, with each edge depicted as a pair of vertices. This method is simple and direct.

2. Directed Graph: In this context, each edge is directed and is denoted as a tuple (u, v), signifying a connection from vertex u to vertex v.

3. Weighted Graph: Each edge can also be expressed in the form (u, v, weight), incorporating the weight associated with the edge.

4. Space Complexity: The space complexity is O(E).

Example:

python

```
# Edge list for an undirected graph
edge_list = [
(0, 1),
(1, 2),
(1, 3),
(2, 3)
]
```

4. Incidence Matrix

- The structure is represented as a two-dimensional array, where the rows correspond to vertices and the columns correspond to edges. The entry at position (i,j) indicates whether vertex i is associated with edge j.
- For undirected graphs, the matrix will display a value of 1 if the vertex is linked to the edge, and 0 if it is not.

In the case of directed graphs, the matrix can exhibit the following values:

- 1 if the vertex serves as the source of the edge.
- -1 if the vertex acts as the target of the edge.
- 0 if there is no connection between the vertex and the edge.
- The space complexity of this representation is O(V×E).

Graph Traversal

Graph traversals are fundamental methods employed to navigate through the nodes of a graph. The two predominant algorithms for traversal are Depth-First Search (DFS) and Breadth-First Search (BFS). Each algorithm possesses distinct features and is suited for specific scenarios. Below is a comprehensive examination of both techniques, encompassing their algorithms, implementations, and practical applications.

1. Depth-First Search (DFS)

Overview:

Depth-First Search (DFS) investigates each branch to its fullest extent before retracing its steps. It employs a stack, which may be implemented explicitly or through recursion, to monitor the nodes that remain to be explored.

Algorithm:

1. Start at the root (or an arbitrary node).
2. Mark the node as visited.
3. Explore each adjacent unvisited node, recursively applying DFS.
4. Backtrack when no unvisited adjacent nodes remain.

Implementation:

- **Using Recursion:**

```
Python
def depth_first_search(graph, current_node, visited_nodes):
if current_node not in visited_nodes:
visited_nodes.add(current_node)
print(current_node) # Process the current node (e.g., print it)
for adjacent in graph[current_node]:
depth_first_search(graph, adjacent, visited_nodes)
# Example usage
graph_structure = {
0: [1, 2],
1: [0, 3, 4],
2: [0],
3: [1],
4: [1]
}
visited_set = set()
depth_first_search(graph_structure, 0, visited_set)
```

- **Using an Explicit Stack:**

```
Python
def iterative_dfs(graph, start_node):
visited_nodes = set()
node_stack = [start_node]
while node_stack:
current_node = node_stack.pop()
if current_node not in visited_nodes:
visited_nodes.add(current_node)
print(current_node) # Process the current node
node_stack.extend(neighbor for neighbor in graph[current_node] if neighbor not in visited_nodes)
```

```
# Example usage
iterative_dfs(graph, 0)
```

2. Breadth-First Search (BFS)

Overview:

Breadth-First Search (BFS) systematically examines all neighboring nodes at the current depth before advancing to nodes at the subsequent depth level. It employs a queue to manage the nodes awaiting exploration.

Algorithm:

1. Begin at the root node (or any chosen node).
2. Mark the node as visited and add it to the queue.
3. Continue the process while the queue remains populated:

- Remove a node from the front of the queue.
- Process the node (for instance, by printing it).
- Add all adjacent unvisited nodes to the queue, marking them as visited.

Implementation:

Python

```
from collections import deque
def breadth_first_search(graph, start_node):
visited_nodes = set()
node_queue = deque([start_node])
visited_nodes.add(start_node)
while node_queue:
current_node = node_queue.popleft()
print(current_node) # Process the current node
for adjacent_node in graph[current_node]:
if adjacent_node not in visited_nodes:
visited_nodes.add(adjacent_node)
node_queue.append(adjacent_node)
# Example usage
breadth_first_search(graph, 0)
```

Applications of Graph Traversals

- **DFS Applications:**
  - Topological sorting (for directed acyclic graphs).
  - Finding connected components in undirected graphs.
  - Solving puzzles (e.g., maze solving).
  - Pathfinding algorithms.

Depth-First Search (DFS) is a highly adaptable algorithm that finds utility across numerous domains. Below are several significant applications:

1. Topological Sorting

- **Description**: In directed acyclic graphs (DAGs), depth-first search (DFS) can be employed to generate a linear sequence of vertices, ensuring that for each directed edge u→vu \rightarrow vu→v, vertex u precedes vertex v in the sequence.
- **Use Case**: Scheduling tasks or course prerequisites.

2. Finding Connected Components

- **Description**: In undirected graphs, DFS can help identify connected components by marking all reachable vertices from a starting vertex.
- **Use Case**: Analyzing social networks or clustering in data mining.

3. Cycle Detection

- **Description**: DFS can be used to detect cycles in both directed and undirected graphs. For directed graphs, it checks for back edges; for undirected graphs, it looks for edges leading to already visited vertices that are not the direct parent.
- **Use Case**: Verifying acyclic properties in dependency graphs.

4. Pathfinding

- **Description**: DFS can be utilized to find paths between nodes, although it doesn't guarantee the shortest path in weighted graphs.
- **Use Case**: Solving mazes or games where multiple paths may be explored.

5. Backtracking Algorithms

- **Description**: DFS is often employed in backtracking problems, exploring possible solutions and abandoning paths that lead to dead ends.
- **Use Case**: N-Queens problem, Sudoku solver, or generating permutations and combinations.

6. Solving Puzzles

- **Description**: DFS can explore all possible configurations in puzzles, like the Rubik's cube or sliding tile puzzles.
- **Use Case**: Game AI to determine moves or configurations.

7. Artificial Intelligence and Game Theory

- **Description**: DFS is used in decision trees to explore potential moves and outcomes.
- **Use Case**: Implementing algorithms for games like chess or tic-tac-toe.

8. Web Crawling

- **Description**: DFS can be used to traverse web pages by following links.
- **Use Case**: Search engines exploring the web to index content.

9. Finding Strongly Connected Components

- **Description**: In directed graphs, Tarjan's or Kosaraju's algorithm uses DFS to identify strongly connected components (subsets where Every vertex can be accessed from any other vertex).
- **Use Case**: Analyzing network connectivity and dependencies.

10. Network Flow Problems

- **Description**: DFS can be part of algorithms that find augmenting paths in flow networks, like the Ford-Fulkerson method.
- **Use Case**: Optimizing network traffic or resource allocation.
    -

- **BFS Applications**:
    - Finding the shortest path in unweighted graphs.
    - Level order traversal of trees.
    - Network broadcasting in communication networks.
    - Finding connected components in undirected graphs.

- **Breadth-First Search (BFS)** is a prominent algorithm utilized for traversing graphs, offering a variety of practical applications. Below are some of the most prevalent uses of BFS:

1. **Shortest Path in Unweighted Graphs**:

- Description: BFS is capable of determining the shortest path, measured by the number of edges, from a designated starting node to all other nodes within an unweighted graph.
- **Use Case**: Navigating in maps or social networks where all connections have the same weight.

2. Finding Connected Components

- **Description**: Like DFS, BFS can be used to identify connected components in an undirected graph by marking all reachable nodes from a starting node.

- **Use Case**: Analyzing groups in social networks or identifying clusters in data.

3. Level Order Traversal of Trees

- **Description**: BFS explores nodes level by level, making it useful for traversing trees in a breadth-first manner.
- **Use Case**: Printing nodes of a binary tree level by level, useful in visual representations of trees.

4. Web Crawling:

• **Overview**: Breadth-First Search (BFS) is employed in web crawlers to navigate through web pages by tracing hyperlinks, guaranteeing that all pages at a specific "depth" are accessed prior to delving further.

• **Application:** Cataloging websites for search engines, thereby ensuring thorough coverage of all hyperlinks.

5. Broadcasting in Networks

- **Description**: BFS can simulate broadcasting messages in a network by exploring all neighboring nodes before moving to the next level of nodes.
- **Use Case**: Sending updates in computer networks or peer-to-peer systems.

6. Finding the Minimum Spanning Tree

- **Description**: While BFS itself doesn't find minimum spanning trees, variations of it (like Prim's algorithm) leverage BFS concepts.
- **Use Case**: Network design where minimizing connection costs is essential.

7. Finding Bipartite Graphs

- **Description**: BFS can be employed to determine whether a graph is bipartite by attempting to color the graph with two distinct colors during the traversal process.
- **Use Case**: Scheduling problems or resource allocation where tasks can be divided into two distinct groups.

8. AI and Game Development

- **Description**: BFS can be employed in AI algorithms to explore game states or search trees.
- **Use Case**: Implementing AI opponents in games where breadth-first exploration is needed to evaluate moves.

9. Social Network Analysis

- **Description**: BFS can be used to determine the degrees of separation between users in social networks.
- **Use Case**: Finding how closely related two individuals are based on their connections.

10. Network Flow Algorithms

- **Description**: BFS is part of the Edmonds-Karp algorithm, which finds maximum flow in flow networks using the Ford-Fulkerson method.
- **Use Case**: Optimizing resource allocation in logistics or transportation systems.

Complexity:

- **Time Complexity**:

- Both Depth-First Search (DFS) and Breadth-First Search (BFS) traverse each vertex and edge a single time, leading to a time complexity of O (V + E), where V represents the number of vertices and E denotes the number of edges.

- The time complexity of these graph traversal algorithms can be analyzed based on the graph's structure. Below is a detailed explanation of their complexities.

1. Time Complexity of DFS

- Time Complexity: O(V + E)
- V: Represents the total number of vertices (or nodes) within the graph.
- E: Denotes the total number of edges present in the graph.

Explanation:

- Each vertex is examined precisely one time, and for every vertex, all of its neighboring edges are investigated.
- This leads to a linear time complexity in relation to the graph's size.

2. Time Complexity of BFS:

- Time Complexity: O(V + E)
- V: Represents the total number of vertices in the graph.
- E: Denotes the total number of edges in the graph.

Explanation:

- Similar to DFS, BFS visits each vertex once and examines all of its edges.
- The overall complexity remains linear with respect to the graph size.

Additional Considerations

- **Graph Representation:**

1. Adjacency List: Both Depth-First Search (DFS) and Breadth-First Search (BFS) demonstrate high efficiency when utilizing adjacency lists, as these structures facilitate rapid access to neighboring nodes, thereby maintaining a complexity of O(V + E).

2. Adjacency Matrix: Conversely, when employing an adjacency matrix, the time complexity for edge lookups is O(1); however, traversing all vertices results in a complexity of O(V^2). Consequently, both traversal methods can exhibit a complexity of O(V^2) when an adjacency matrix is used.

- **Space Complexity**:
    - DFS (recursive): O(h) for the call stack, where hhh is the maximum height of the tree (could be O(V)O(V)O(V) in the worst case).
    - DFS (iterative): O(V) for the stack.
    - BFS: O(V) for the queue.

The space complexity associated with graph traversal algorithms, particularly Depth-First Search (DFS) and Breadth-First Search (BFS), is influenced by the implementation technique and the graph's structure. Below is an analysis:

1. Space Complexity of DFS

Recursive Implementation:

- Space Complexity: O(h)
- h: Represents the maximum height of the recursion stack.
- In the worst-case scenario (such as in a skewed tree or graph), h can reach O(V), where V denotes the number of vertices.

The recursive approach to implementing graph traversal algorithms, especially Depth-First Search (DFS), is widely recognized for its elegance and effectiveness. The following provides a comprehensive overview of how to execute DFS recursively, accompanied by an illustrative example.

Recursive DFS Implementation

Overview

In the recursive approach, the function calls itself for each adjacent unvisited vertex, effectively creating a call stack that mimics the behavior of an explicit stack used in the iterative version.

Algorithm Steps

1. Start at a given vertex (source node).
2. Mark the vertex as visited.
3. Process the vertex (e.g., print its value).
4. For each adjacent unvisited vertex, call the DFS function recursively.

Implementation Example

A Python implementation of recursive Depth-First Search (DFS) utilizing an adjacency list representation is provided below:

```
```python
def dfs_recursive(graph, node, visited):
# Mark the current node as visited
visited.add(node)
print(node) # Process the node (e.g., print it)
# Recur for all vertices adjacent to this vertex
for neighbor in graph[node]:
if neighbor not in visited:
dfs_recursive(graph, neighbor, visited)
# Example usage
graph = {
0: [1, 2],
1: [0, 3, 4],
2: [0],
3: [1],
4: [1]
}
visited = set() # Set to track visited nodes
```
```

```
dfs_recursive(graph, 0, visited)
```

Explanation of the Code

- **Function Parameters:**
  - graph: The adjacency list representing the graph.
  - node: The current vertex being visited.
  - visited: A set to track visited vertices, preventing cycles.
- **Process:**
  - The function starts by marking the current node as visited.
  - It then prints the node (or processes it in another way).
  - The function iterates through all neighbors of the current node and calls itself recursively for any unvisited neighbor.
- Base Case: The recursion concludes when there are no remaining unvisited adjacent nodes.
- Space Complexity: The space complexity associated with the recursive implementation is O(h), where h represents the maximum height of the recursion stack. In the most unfavorable scenario, this can escalate to O(V) for a graph structure that is deeply nested.
- Time Complexity: The time complexity is consistently O(V + E), as each vertex and edge is traversed precisely once.

Iterative Implementation:

- Space Complexity: O(V)
- This is attributed to the stack utilized for storing the vertices that require exploration. In the worst-case scenario, it is possible for all vertices to be held in the stack.
- The iterative implementation of Depth-First Search (DFS) uses an explicit stack to manage the traversal process, rather than

relying on the call stack used in the recursive approach. This method can be more suitable for deep graphs, as it avoids potential stack overflow issues. Here's how to implement DFS iteratively:

Iterative DFS Implementation:

Overview:

In the iterative method, a stack is employed to monitor the vertices that require exploration. The process persists until the stack is devoid of elements.

Algorithm Steps:

1. Begin at a specified vertex (source node) and place it onto the stack.

2. As long as the stack contains elements:

- Remove the vertex at the top of the stack.
- If this vertex has not been visited, designate it as visited and carry out the necessary processing.
- Add all adjacent vertices that have not yet been visited to the stack.

Implementation Example:

Here's a Python implementation of iterative DFS using an adjacency list representation:

```
def dfs_iterative(graph, start):
visited_nodes = set() # Set to track nodes that have been visited
node_stack = [start] # Initialize the stack with the starting node
while node_stack:
current_node = node_stack.pop() # Retrieve the top node from the stack
if current_node not in visited_nodes:
visited_nodes.add(current_node) # Mark the current node as visited
print(current_node) # Process the current node (e.g., print it)
# Add all unvisited adjacent nodes to the stack
```

```
for adjacent in reversed(graph[current_node]): # Reverse for correct order
if adjacent not in visited_nodes:
node_stack.append(adjacent)
# Example usage
graph = {
0: [1, 2],
1: [0, 3, 4],
2: [0],
3: [1],
4: [1]
}
dfs_iterative(graph, 0)
```

Explanation of the Code

- **Function Parameters**:
  - graph: The adjacency list representing the graph.
  - start: The starting vertex for the DFS traversal.
- **Process**:
  - A stack is initialized with the starting node.
  - The algorithm enters a loop that continues until the stack is empty.
  - The top node is popped from the stack. If it has not been visited, it is marked as visited and processed (e.g., printed).
  - All unvisited adjacent nodes are pushed onto the stack. The neighbors are reversed to maintain the correct order of traversal since stacks are LIFO (Last In, First Out).

Key Points

- **Space Complexity:** The iterative implementation exhibits a space complexity of O(V) because of the stack utilized for storing the nodes.

- **Time Complexity**: The time complexity is consistently O(V + E), as each vertex and edge is visited precisely one time.
- **Order of Traversal:** The sequence of traversal may vary slightly from that of the recursive version, influenced by the behavior of the stack and the manner in which neighbors are added.

2. Space Complexity of BFS
• Space Complexity: O(V)

- **Breadth-First Search (BFS)** employs a queue to manage the vertices awaiting exploration. In the most unfavorable scenario, it is possible for all vertices to be held in the queue at the same time.
- The space complexity of the iterative version of Depth-First Search (DFS) can be evaluated by considering the data structures utilized and the properties of the graph being navigated. Below is a comprehensive analysis:

Space Complexity of Iterative DFS:

1. **Stack for Traversal**:

- The main factor influencing space complexity is the explicit stack utilized to maintain the vertices that require exploration.
- In the most unfavorable scenario, the stack could contain all the vertices of the graph, especially in instances of a deep or linear configuration, such as a linked list. Space Complexity:
- O(V), where V represents the number of vertices in the graph.

1. **Visited Set**:

- An auxiliary data structure, commonly a set or a boolean array, is generally employed to monitor the vertices that have been visited, thereby avoiding cycles and redundant processing.

- Space Complexity: O(V)
- This accounts for all vertices in the worst-case scenario.

Total Space Complexity:

Combining both components, the total space complexity for the iterative DFS implementation is:

Total Space Complexity: O(V)

Additional Considerations:

Graph Representation:

- When employing an adjacency list to represent the graph, the space complexity is O(V + E), where E denotes the number of edges. It is important to note that this representation is distinct from the space complexity associated with the DFS algorithm itself.
- In contrast, if an adjacency matrix is utilized, the space complexity becomes O(V^2), which similarly does not have a direct impact on the space complexity of the traversal.

Summary:

Iterative Depth-First Search (DFS) exhibits the following characteristics:

- The main space complexity is O(V) due to the utilization of the stack and the visited structure.
- In terms of space efficiency, the traversal is superior to that of recursive DFS, where the recursion stack can also attain a depth of O(V).

Additional Considerations

Graph Representation:

- The space complexity associated with storing the graph using an adjacency list is O(V + E), where E represents the number of edges. This holds true for both Depth-First Search (DFS) and Breadth-First Search (BFS).

- An **adjacency list** is a widely used data structure for representing graphs. It is efficient in terms of both space and time, particularly for sparse graphs. Here's an overview of the adjacency list, including its structure, advantages, disadvantages, and examples.

Structure of Adjacency List

In an adjacency list representation:

• Each vertex within the graph is associated with a list that includes its adjacent vertices (neighbors).

• This representation can be realized through an array of lists, a dictionary of lists, or a comparable structure, depending on the programming language utilized.

Example:

For a graph with the following edges:

- 0 — 1
- 0 — 2
- 1 — 2
- 1 — 3
- 2 — 4

The adjacency list representation would look like this:

```
python
graph = {
0: [1, 2],
1: [0, 2, 3],
2: [0, 1, 4],
3: [1],
4: [2]
}
```

Advantages of Adjacency List

1. Space Efficiency:

For sparse graphs, characterized by a significantly lower number of edges (E) compared to the square of the number of vertices (V^2), adjacency lists demonstrate superior space efficiency over adjacency matrices, utilizing O (V + E) space.

2. Dynamic Edge Insertion:

The process of adding or removing edges is efficient, as it necessitates merely updating the lists associated with the relevant vertices.

3. Iterating Over Neighbors:

Iterating through the neighbors of a vertex is a straightforward task, which is frequently required in various graph algorithms.

Disadvantages of Adjacency List

1. Access Time:

- The process of verifying the presence of a specific edge may be less efficient in an adjacency list compared to an adjacency matrix, where the existence of an edge can be determined in constant time, O (1).
- In contrast, an adjacency list necessitates a search through the list, which can result in a time complexity of O(V) in the worst-case scenario.

2. Complexity for Dense Graphs:

- In the case of dense graphs, where the number of edges E approaches V squared (V^2), adjacency matrices can prove to be more space-efficient.
- This is due to the potential complications arising from the need to maintain lists for each vertex, which can introduce unnecessary complexity.

Summary

- An adjacency list serves as a compact representation of graphs, making it particularly advantageous for sparse graphs.

- The space complexity associated with this structure is O (V + E). The time complexity for various operations is as follows: iterating through all neighbors of a vertex takes O(V) for each vertex; adding or removing edges is performed in O (1) on average for lists; and checking for the presence of an edge requires O(V) through a linear search.
- In contrast, the adjacency matrix representation has a space complexity of $O(V^2)$, which remains constant regardless of the algorithm employed.
- The adjacency list is a prevalent data structure for graph representation, offering efficiency in both space and time, especially in the context of sparse graphs. This overview encompasses its structure, benefits, drawbacks, and illustrative examples.

Structure of Adjacency List

In an adjacency list representation:

- Each vertex in the graph has a list (or a collection) that contains its adjacent vertices (neighbors).
- This can be implemented using an array (or list) of lists, a dictionary of lists, or a similar structure depending on the programming language.

Example

For a graph with the following edges:

- 0 — 1
- 0 — 2
- 1 — 2
- 1 — 3
- 2 — 4

The adjacency list representation would look like this:

python

```
graph = {
0: [1, 2],
1: [0, 2, 3],
2: [0, 1, 4],
3: [1],
4: [2]
}
```

Advantages of Adjacency List

1. Space Efficiency:

For sparse graphs, characterized by a significantly lower number of edges (E) compared to the square of the number of vertices (V^2), adjacency lists demonstrate superior space efficiency over adjacency matrices, utilizing $O(V + E)$ space.

2. Dynamic Edge Insertion:

The process of adding or removing edges is efficient, as it necessitates merely updating the lists associated with the relevant vertices.

3. Iterating Over Neighbors:

Iterating through the neighbors of a vertex is a straightforward task, which is frequently required in various graph algorithms.

Disadvantages of Adjacency List:

1. Access Time:

The process of verifying the presence of a specific edge may be less efficient in an adjacency list compared to an adjacency matrix, where the existence of an edge can be determined in constant time, $O(1)$. In contrast, an adjacency list necessitates a search through the list, which can result in a time complexity of $O(V)$ in the worst-case scenario.

2. Complexity for Dense Graphs:

In the case of dense graphs, where the number of edges (E) approaches the square of the number of vertices (V^2), adjacency matrices can prove to be more space-efficient. This is due to the potential complications arising from the need to maintain lists for each vertex, which can introduce unnecessary complexity.

Summary

- **Adjacency List:** A space-efficient way to represent graphs, particularly useful for sparse graphs.

- Space Complexity: O (V + E)
- Time Complexity for Operations:
- Iterating through all adjacent vertices: O(V) for each vertex.
- Adding or deleting edges: O (1) (amortized for lists).
- Verifying the presence of an edge: O(V) (linear search).

A Directed Acyclic Graph (DAG) is a framework utilized in the fields of computer science and mathematics, characterized by a collection of nodes and directed edges, with the absence of cycles. This implies that it is impossible to begin at a particular node and traverse a path that ultimately returns to that same node.DAGs are commonly used in various applications, including:

Directed Acyclic Graphs (DAGs) find extensive application across multiple domains, such as:

1. Task Scheduling:

- In the realm of project management, tasks are depicted as nodes, while dependencies are illustrated as directed edges.
- This structure guarantees that prerequisite tasks are finalized prior to the initiation of subsequent tasks.
- The process of task scheduling utilizing **a Directed Acyclic Graph (DAG)entails** arranging interdependent tasks in a manner that ensures all prerequisites are accomplished before any dependent tasks commence. Below is an explanation of the operational framework.

Key Concepts

1. **Nodes and Edges:**

    - **Nodes** represent tasks.

- **Directed edges** indicate dependencies (i.e., Task A must be finalized prior to the commencement of task B.)

2. **Acyclic:**

   - The absence of cycles ensures that there's a clear order of execution without infinite loops.

Steps in Task Scheduling

1. **Define Tasks and Dependencies:**

Identify all tasks and their dependencies. For example, if Task B cannot start until Task A is finished, there will be a directed edge from A to B.

2. Develop the Directed Acyclic Graph (DAG).

Create a graph representation of tasks and their dependencies. Each task becomes a node, and each dependency becomes a directed edge.

3. **Topological Sorting:**

Use algorithms (like Kahn's algorithm or Depth-First Search) to generate a topological order of the tasks. This order ensures that each task appears before any tasks that depend on it.

4. **Schedule Execution:**

Based on the topological order, execute tasks in a way that respects their dependencies. This often involves parallel execution of independent tasks.

Benefits

- **Efficiency**: Helps optimize resource utilization by allowing parallel execution of independent tasks.
- **Clarity**: Visual representation makes it easier to understand task relationships and dependencies.
- **Error Reduction**: Ensures that dependencies are respected, reducing the risk of errors caused by running tasks out of order.

Applications

- **Project Management**: Tools like Gantt charts often represent tasks and dependencies similarly.
- **Data Processing**: Systems like Apache Airflow and Luigi manage data workflows using DAGs to ensure tasks run in the correct order.
- **Build Systems**: Tools like Make and Gradle use DAGs to manage builds based on file dependencies.

1. **Data Processing Pipelines**:

In systems like Apache Airflow, workflows are designed as DAGs to manage data processing tasks with clear dependency chains.

Data processing pipelines often use Directed Acyclic Graphs (DAGs) to manage the flow of data through various transformation and processing stages. Here's an overview of how DAGs are utilized in this context:

Key Components of Data Processing Pipelines:

1. **Nodes**:

    - Each node represents a specific processing step or operation, such as data extraction, transformation, or loading (ETL).

2. **Edges**:

  - Directed edges signify the flow of data from one step to the next, indicating dependencies between tasks.

How DAGs Function in Data Processing:

1. **Defining the Pipeline**:
   - Identify the data sources, processing steps, and final outputs. Each processing task becomes a node in the DAG, with edges showing how data flows from one task to another.
2. **Creating the DAG**:
   - Construct the DAG based on the defined tasks and their dependencies. This ensures that each step follows the appropriate order and that no cyclic dependencies exist.
3. **Execution**:
   - The pipeline is executed according to the DAG structure. Tasks can often run in parallel if they have no dependencies on each other, improving efficiency.
4. **Monitoring and Management**:
   - Tools designed for managing data pipelines often provide features for monitoring task execution, handling failures, and retrying tasks as needed.

Advantages of Using DAGs:

- **Parallelism**: Allows independent tasks to run simultaneously, optimizing resource use and reducing overall processing time.
- **Clear Dependency Management**: Makes it easy to visualize and manage task dependencies, which can be crucial for debugging

and maintaining data integrity.

- **Scalability**: Pipelines can be scaled by adding more nodes for additional processing steps without disrupting the overall structure.

Common Tools and Frameworks:

Several tools and frameworks utilize DAGs for data processing:

- **Apache Airflow**: A platform for programmatically authoring, scheduling, and monitoring workflows using DAGs.
- **Luigi**: A Python module that helps build complex pipelines of batch jobs, managing dependencies and workflows with a DAG structure.
- **Apache NiFi**: A tool for automating the flow of data between systems, using a DAG-like model for data routing and transformation.

Real-World Use Cases:

- **ETL Processes**: Extracting data from various sources, transforming it to fit operational needs, and loading it into data warehouses or databases.
- **Machine Learning Pipelines**: Managing the flow of data through different stages, from data preprocessing to model training and evaluation.
- **Data Integration**: Combining data from multiple sources while ensuring that transformations occur in the correct order.

2. **Blockchain**:

Some cryptocurrencies use a DAG structure to allow for more efficient transactions compared to traditional blockchain models.

In blockchain technology, Directed Acyclic Graphs (DAGs) are used as an alternative structure to traditional linear blockchains. Here's how they work and their advantages:

Key Concepts of DAG in Blockchain:

1. **Nodes:**
   - Each node in a DAG represents a transaction rather than a block of transactions, as seen in traditional blockchains.
2. **Directed Edges:**
   - Each edge points from one transaction to another, indicating that the later transaction confirms the earlier one. This creates a directed path without cycles.

How DAGs Function in Blockchain:

1. **Transaction Confirmation:**
   - In a DAG-based blockchain, each new transaction references one or more previous transactions, providing confirmation for them. This creates a network of interconnected transactions.
2. **Parallel Processing:**
   - Because transactions can be confirmed independently, multiple transactions can be processed simultaneously. This allows for greater scalability compared to traditional blockchains, where blocks must be added in a linear fashion.
3. **No Miners Needed:**
   - Many DAG-based systems do not require miners in the same way traditional blockchains do. Instead, users validate transactions by confirming previous ones, reducing the need for intensive computational work.

Advantages of Using DAGs in Blockchain:

- **Scalability**: DAGs can handle a high volume of transactions simultaneously, making them suitable for applications requiring rapid processing.
- **Lower Fees**: Since there's no need for mining rewards, transaction fees can be significantly lower.
- **Fast Confirmation Times**: Transactions can be confirmed more quickly, as they do not have to wait for a block to be mined.

Examples of DAG-Based Blockchains:

- **IOTA**: Utilizes a DAG called the Tangle, where each transaction confirms two previous transactions, promoting fast and feeless transactions ideal for IoT applications.
- **Hashgraph**: A distributed ledger technology that uses a gossip protocol for fast consensus and high transaction throughput.
- **Nano**: Uses a block-lattice structure, where each account has its own blockchain, enabling quick and free transactions.

Use Cases:

- **Internet of Things (IoT)**: Ideal for environments requiring high transaction rates and low fees, like smart device communication.
- **Microtransactions**: Supports applications where small transactions occur frequently, such as tipping or pay-per-use services.
- **Supply Chain Management**: Enables tracking and validating transactions in real-time across multiple participants without bottlenecks.

3. **Version Control Systems:**

Systems like Git use a DAG to manage commits, where each commit points to its parent(s), creating a history of changes without cycles.

Version control systems (VCS) often use Directed Acyclic Graphs (DAGs) to manage changes to files and track the history of development projects. Here's a closer look at how DAGs are utilized in version control:

Key Concepts in Version Control Systems:

1. **Commits as Nodes:**
    - Each commit represents a snapshot of the project at a specific point in time, functioning as a node in the DAG.
2. **Directed Edges:**
    - Directed edges connect commits, indicating the parent-child relationships. A commit points to its parent commit(s), showing how changes evolve over time.

How DAGs Function in Version Control:

1. **Creating a Commit:**
    - When changes are made to a project, they are staged and then committed. Each commit contains a reference to its parent commit, creating a directed edge.
2. **Branching and Merging:**
    - Branches are effectively separate paths in the DAG. When a branch is merged, a new commit is created that references the latest commits from both branches, preserving the history of changes.
3. **History Tracking:**

- The DAG structure allows users to navigate the history of changes easily, reviewing past versions and understanding how the project has evolved.

Advantages of Using DAGs in Version Control:

- **Non-linear History:** Facilitates intricate workflows through branching and merging, enabling multiple developers to collaborate on features concurrently without the risk of overwriting one another's contributions.
- **Effective Conflict Resolution:** The Directed Acyclic Graph (DAG) structure aids in recognizing and addressing conflicts during branch merging by utilizing the shared history.
- **Versatile Navigation:** Users have the capability to examine the commit history, revert to earlier versions, or initiate new branches from any given commit.

Popular Version Control Systems:

1. **Git:**
    - Uses a DAG to represent commits and their relationships, enabling powerful features like branching, merging, and rebasing.
2. **Mercurial:**
    - Similar to Git, it also utilizes a DAG structure to manage changes and provides robust support for branching and merging.
3. **Bazaar:**
    - Another distributed version control system that employs a DAG to track changes, making collaboration straightforward.

Use Cases:

- **Software Development**: Allows teams to collaborate on code, manage feature development, and maintain different versions of a project.
- **Document Versioning**: Useful in environments where multiple revisions of documents need to be tracked and managed over time.
- **Configuration Management**: Helps in maintaining configurations for applications or systems, enabling rollback and audit trails.

Topological ordering is a technique used with Directed Acyclic Graphs (DAGs) to arrange the nodes in a linear sequence that respects the direction of edges. In simpler terms, it provides a way to list the nodes such that for every directed edge from node AAA to node BBB, node AAA appears before node BBB in the ordering.

Key Concepts

1. **DAG Requirement**:

    - Topological ordering can only be performed on a DAG, as the presence of cycles would make it impossible to establish a linear order.

The requirement that a graph be a Directed Acyclic Graph (DAG) for topological ordering is crucial due to the following reasons:

Directed:

- **Direction of Edges**: In a directed acyclic graph (DAG), the edges possess a specific orientation, indicating that they connect one vertex (or node) to another in a defined manner. This directional characteristic is crucial for delineating a distinct relationship among the nodes.

- **Dependency Representation**: Directed edges represent dependencies, allowing you to see which tasks must be completed before others can start. In a topological ordering, you want to ensure that for every directed edge from node AAA to node BBB, AAA appears before BBB.

Acyclic:

- **No Cycles**: A DAG has no cycles, meaning you cannot start at one node and follow a path that eventually loops back to the same node. This is vital for topological ordering because:

- **No Conflicts**: Allowing cycles would result in conflicting dependencies, thereby preventing the establishment of a consistent sequence. For example, if Task A relies on Task B, while Task B simultaneously relies on Task A, it becomes impossible to ascertain the order in which the tasks should be executed.

- **Feasibility of Ordering**: The acyclic property guarantees that it is always possible to find a valid linear sequence of nodes that satisfies all dependencies.

Implications for Topological Ordering:

- **Existence**: A topological order exists only for DAGs. If a graph has cycles, it cannot be topologically sorted, as there would be no way to order the nodes without violating dependency constraints.
- **Algorithm Applicability**: Algorithms for topological sorting (like Kahn's algorithm or DFS) specifically rely on the properties of DAGs to function correctly. These algorithms would fail or enter an infinite loop if cycles were present.
    -

1. **Applications:**

    - Commonly used in scheduling tasks, resolving dependencies (like in package management), and representing workflows.
    -

Algorithms for Topological Ordering

Several algorithms can be used to obtain a topological order of a DAG:

1. **Kahn's Algorithm:**

    - **Initialization:** Start with a list of nodes that have no incoming edges (in-degree of zero).
    - **Process:**

        - Remove a node from this list and add it to the topological order.
        - For each outgoing edge from this node, reduce the in-degree of the connected nodes. If any of those nodes' in-degrees become zero, add them to the list.

    - **Repeat** until all nodes are processed.

Kahn's Algorithm is a commonly employed technique for executing topological sorting on a Directed Acyclic Graph (DAG). This algorithm is characterized by its efficiency, operating by systematically eliminating nodes that possess no incoming edges (i.e., an in-degree of zero) and subsequently adjusting the in-degrees of their adjacent nodes. Below is a detailed, step-by-step explanation of the functioning of Kahn's Algorithm.

Steps of Kahn's Algorithm:

1. **Initialization:**

1. Calculate In-Degrees: Establish an array to monitor the in-degrees of each node, where the in-degree signifies the count of edges directed towards that particular node.

2. Construct the Graph: Utilize an adjacency list or an appropriate data structure to represent the graph.

3. Initialize the Queue: Set up a queue (or list) containing all nodes that possess an in-degree of zero.

2. **Processing Nodes:**

As long as the queue remains populated:

- Remove a node (designated as uuu) from the queue and append it to the list representing the topological order.
- For every adjacent node vvv that uuu connects to:
- Reduce the in-degree of vvv by 1 (due to the removal of uuu).
- If the in-degree of vvv reaches zero, add vvv to the queue.

3. **Check for Cycles:**

If the quantity of nodes incorporated into the topological order is fewer than the overall number of nodes in the graph, it indicates that the graph contains at least one cycle, thereby preventing the formation of a valid topological order.

4. **Output the Result:**

    - If the topological order contains all nodes, return it. Otherwise, indicate that the graph is not a DAG.

Pseudocode:

Here's a simple pseudocode representation of Kahn's Algorithm:

Plaintext

function KahnTopologicalSort(graph):

inDegree = array of size |V| initialized to 0

```
for each vertex in graph:
for each adjacent vertex of vertex:
inDegree[adjacent] += 1
queue = empty queue
for each vertex in graph:
if inDegree[vertex] == 0:
enqueue queue, vertex)
topologicalOrder = empty list
while queue is not empty:
u = dequeue(queue)
add u to topologicalOrder
for each adjacent vertex v of u:
inDegree[v] -= 1
if inDegree[v] == 0:
enqueue (queue, v)
if length of topologicalOrder! =|V|:
return "Graph contains a cycle"
return topologicalOrder
```

Complexity:

- **Time Complexity**: O (V + E), where V represents the number of vertices (or nodes) and E denotes the number of edges. This complexity arises from the fact that each vertex and edge is examined a single time.
- **Space Complexity:** O(V) is required for maintaining the in-degree counts and the topological order.

Advantages of Kahn's Algorithm:

- **Iterative Approach**: Unlike DFS-based methods, Kahn's Algorithm uses an iterative approach, which can be easier to understand and implement in some contexts.
- **Cycle Detection**: It can detect cycles in the graph, which is crucial for determining whether a valid topological order exists.

2. **Depth-First Search (DFS)**:
   - Perform a DFS traversal on the graph:
     - Mark nodes as visited.
     - Recursively visit all unvisited adjacent nodes.
     - After exploring all adjacent nodes of a node, push it onto a stack.
   - The topological order is obtained by popping nodes from the stack.

Depth-First Search (DFS) is a widely utilized technique for executing topological sorting on a Directed Acyclic Graph (DAG). This algorithm delves deeply into each branch before retracing its steps, thereby effectively identifying the dependencies among nodes. The process of topological sorting using DFS can be outlined in a series of steps:Steps of DFS-Based Topological Sorting:

1. **Initialization**:
   - Create a stack to store the topological order.
   - Create a set or array to track visited nodes to avoid processing the same node multiple times.
2. **DFS Function**:

   For every node within the graph that has yet to be visited:

- Designate the node as visited.
- Recursively explore all neighboring nodes that have not been visited (i.e., for each adjacent node).
- Once all neighboring nodes have been explored, place the current node onto the stack.

3. **Construct the Topological Order**:
    - Once all nodes have been processed, the stack will contain the nodes in reverse topological order. To get the correct order, pop nodes from the stack.
4. **Output the Result**:
    - The nodes popped from the stack represent the topological order of the DAG.

Pseudocode:

Here's a simple pseudocode representation of the DFS-based topological sort:

Plaintext

```
function DFS(node, visited, stack):
visited[node] = true
for each neighbor in graph[node]:
if not visited[neighbor]:
DFS(neighbor, visited, stack)
stack.push(node)
function TopologicalSort(graph):
stack = new empty stack
visited = new array of size |V| initialized to false
for each node in graph:
if not visited[node]:
DFS(node, visited, stack)
topologicalOrder = new empty list
while not stack.isEmpty():
topologicalOrder.append(stack.pop())
return topologicalOrder
```

Complexity:

- **Time Complexity**:

The time complexity for both Kahn's Algorithm and the Depth-First Search (DFS) approach to topological sorting is O(V + E), where V represents the number of vertices (or nodes) and E denotes the number of edges. Each vertex and edge is processed a single time.

Breakdown of Time Complexity:

1. **Graph Traversal**:

In both algorithms, each vertex is processed precisely one time, resulting in a contribution of O(V) to the overall time complexity.

2. **Edge Processing**:

    - Each edge is also processed exactly once. For example, when updating in-degrees in Kahn's Algorithm or when exploring neighbors in the DFS method, every edge contributes to the overall complexity, adding O(E)O(E)O(E).

Overall Complexity:

Combining these two contributions gives us the total time complexity of O(V+E)O(V + E)O(V+E).

Space Complexity:

In addition to time complexity, it's worth noting the space complexity for both methods:

- Kahn's Algorithm necessitates memory allocation for the storage of node in-degrees and the queue, leading to a space complexity of O(V).
- Conversely, the Depth-First Search (DFS) method requires space for the visited array and the recursion stack (or an explicit stack), which similarly results in a space complexity of O(V).

- **Space Complexity**:

- The notation O(V)O(V)O(V) pertains to the memory utilized for storing the nodes that have been visited, as well as for the stack.
- Space complexity quantifies the total memory space an algorithm necessitates in relation to the size of the input data. This encompasses both the memory allocated for the input data itself and any supplementary memory utilized by the algorithm, such as variables, data structures, and the recursion stack.

Space complexity can be categorized into two components:

1. Fixed Part: This includes the memory required for constants, simple variables, fixed-size variables, and the program code, which remains constant regardless of the input size.

2. Variable Part: This encompasses the memory needed for dynamically allocated resources, the recursion stack, and variable-sized data structures, which is contingent upon the size of the input.

Space complexity is typically expressed using Big O notation, such as:

- **O(1)**: Constant space (e.g., using a fixed number of variables).
- **O(n)**: Linear space (e.g., using an array of size n).
- **O(n^2)**: Quadratic space (e.g., using a 2D array of size n × n).

Advantages of DFS-Based Topological Sorting

- **Simplicity**:

The recursive nature of DFS can make the implementation straightforward and easy to follow.

The simplicity of an algorithm refers to how straightforward and easy it is to understand, implement, and maintain. In the context of topological sorting, both Kahn's Algorithm and the Depth-First Search (DFS) method have their own aspects of simplicity:

Simplicity of Kahn's Algorithm

1. **Iterative Approach:**

   - Kahn's Algorithm uses a queue to manage nodes with no incoming edges, making it intuitive to understand the flow of processing. This iterative method avoids the complexities that can arise with recursion.

2. **Clear Steps:**

   - The algorithm involves distinct steps: calculating in-degrees, processing nodes from the queue, and updating the in-degrees of neighbors. This step-by-step approach makes it easy to follow.

3. **Direct Cycle Detection:**

   - The algorithm is capable of directly identifying the presence of a cycle by verifying whether the count of nodes incorporated into the topological order corresponds to the overall number of nodes within the graph.

Simplicity of DFS-Based Topological Sorting

1. **Recursive Nature:**

   - The recursive implementation of DFS is often more straightforward for those familiar with recursion, leading to a concise code structure. The concept of "visiting" nodes naturally aligns with the recursive calls.

2. **Minimal Data Structures:**

   - The DFS approach typically requires only a stack (or recursion stack) and a visited array, making it simple in terms of data structures used.

3. **Natural Fit for Depth Exploration**:
    - DFS aligns well with the concept of exploring dependencies deeply before backtracking, which can be easier to grasp when visualizing how nodes relate to one another.

- **Flexibility**:

- DFS can easily be adapted for other graph algorithms, such as cycle detection, which can be useful in applications involving graph traversal.
- Flexibility denotes the capacity of a system, process, or method to adjust to alterations or varying circumstances. In different contexts, flexibility may include multiple dimensions.

1. **Software Development**: Flexibility in software means the ease with which code can be modified, extended, or integrated with other systems. This can include modular design, the use of APIs, and the ability to support different configurations or environments.
2. **Business Processes**: A flexible business process can adjust to varying demands, changes in market conditions, or customer needs. This often involves scalable systems and agile methodologies that allow for quick pivots.
3. **Work Environments**: Flexible work environments enable employees to adjust their schedules, work locations, or roles to better suit their personal and professional lives. This can enhance productivity and job satisfaction.
4. **Product Design**: Flexibility in product design refers to the ability to accommodate various user needs and preferences, which can involve customizable features or adaptable designs.

Cycle Detection:

While DFS is used for topological sorting in DAGs, it can also be adapted to detect cycles in the graph. By maintaining an additional set for nodes currently in the recursion stack, the algorithm can identify back edges that indicate cycles.

Cycle detection in a Directed Acyclic Graph (DAG) is crucial for ensuring that topological sorting can be performed. If a graph contains cycles, it's impossible to establish a valid topological order because some nodes would depend on each other in a circular manner. Here's an overview of how cycle detection works in the context of topological sorting, particularly focusing on Kahn's Algorithm and the Depth-First Search (DFS) method.

Cycle Detection Using Kahn's Algorithm:

1. **Initialization:**
    - Compute the in-degrees of all nodes in the graph and initialize a queue with nodes that have an in-degree of zero.
2. **Processing:**
    - As you process each node from the queue:
        - Decrease the in-degrees of its neighbors.
        - If any neighbor's in-degree becomes zero, add it to the queue.
3. **Check for Cycles:**

- Keep track of the total number of nodes incorporated into the topological order. Following the processing phase, if the count of nodes in the topological order is fewer than the overall number of nodes in the graph, it signifies the presence of a cycle.
- This suggests that certain nodes remain unprocessed, indicating their involvement in a cycle.

Cycle Detection Using DFS:

1. **Initialization:**

    - Use a visited array to track visited nodes.
    - Maintain an additional array or set (often called a recursion stack) to track nodes currently in the recursion call stack.

2. **DFS Traversal:**

    - During the DFS traversal, for each node:

        - Designate it as visited and include it in the recursion stack.
        - Recursively visit all unvisited neighbors.
        - After exploring all neighbors, remove the node from the recursion stack.

3. **Check for Back Edges:**

    - If you encounter a neighbor that is already in the recursion stack, a cycle is detected.
    - This back edge indicates that you can reach a previously visited node, confirming a cycle.

Pseudocode for Cycle Detection with DFS:

Here's a simplified version of the DFS-based cycle detection:

Plaintext

```
function DFS (node, visited, recursionStack):
visited[node] = true
recursionStack[node] = true
for each neighbor in graph[node]:
if not visited[neighbor]:
if DFS(neighbor, visited, recursionStack):
return true
else if recursionStack[neighbor]:
return true // Cycle identified
recursionStack[node] = false
```

```
return false
function HasCycle(graph):
visited = array of size |V| initialized to false
recursionStack = array of size |V| initialized to false
for each node in graph:
if not visited[node]:
if DFS (node, visited, recursionStack):
return true
return false
```

Summary:

- **Kahn's Algorithm**: Cycle detection is implicit. If not all nodes are processed due to remaining in-degrees, a cycle exists.
- **DFS Method**: Explicitly tracks the recursion stack to detect back edges, indicating cycles.

Importance of Cycle Detection:

- Ensures the feasibility of topological sorting.
- Helps maintain data integrity in applications like scheduling, dependency resolution, and workflow management.
- Provides insight into the structure of the graph, which can inform design decisions and optimizations.

Cycle detection is a crucial aspect of graph theory and has significant importance in various applications, particularly when dealing with Directed Acyclic Graphs (DAGs). Here's why cycle detection is essential:

1. Ensuring Valid Topological Sorting:

- **Precondition for Topological Order**: Topological sorting can only be performed on DAGs. If a graph contains cycles, it cannot produce a valid linear ordering of nodes that respects their dependencies.

- **Preventing Errors**: Detecting cycles before attempting topological sorting prevents runtime errors and logical inconsistencies in applications.

2. Task and Dependency Management:

- **Project Scheduling**: In project management, tasks often have dependencies. Cycle detection ensures that there are no circular dependencies, which could lead to tasks waiting indefinitely for each other to complete.
- **Build Systems**: In software compilation, cycles in dependencies can cause builds to fail or hang, making cycle detection essential for reliable builds.

3. Data Integrity:

- **Data Processing Workflows**: In data pipelines, cycle detection helps maintain data integrity by ensuring that processing steps do not depend on each other in a circular manner, which could lead to incorrect or incomplete data outputs.
- **Database Operations**: In databases, detecting cycles in foreign key constraints is vital to ensure referential integrity, preventing infinite loops in cascading deletes or updates.

4. Resource Management:

- **Concurrency Control**: In concurrent systems, cycles in resource allocation can lead to deadlocks, where processes wait indefinitely for resources held by each other. Cycle detection in resource allocation graphs can help avoid such scenarios.
- **Distributed Systems**: In distributed systems, detecting cycles in dependency graphs is crucial for maintaining consistency and preventing conflicts.

5. Algorithm Design and Analysis:

- **Graph Algorithms**: Many graph algorithms rely on the absence of cycles (e.g., minimum spanning trees). Cycle detection helps validate input before applying such algorithms, ensuring correct outcomes.
- **Network Design**: In network protocols, cycle detection can help prevent routing loops that can cause network congestion and failure.

6. Debugging and Error Handling:

- **Software Development**: Cycle detection aids in identifying and resolving design flaws, such as circular dependencies in code, which can lead to maintenance challenges and bugs.
- **Configuration Management**: In systems configuration, cycles can lead to inconsistent states. Detecting these cycles allows for corrective measures to be taken before deployment.

Properties:

- **Multiple Orders**:

A DAG can have more than one valid topological order, depending on the traversal method and the graph structure.

In a Directed Acyclic Graph (DAG), multiple valid topological orders can exist due to the inherent flexibility in how nodes are arranged based on their dependencies. Here's a closer look at what this means and its implications:

Understanding Multiple Orders

1. **DAG Structure**:

    - Since a DAG has no cycles and directed edges, it is possible for several arrangements of nodes to respect the dependencies defined by the edges.

2. **Dependencies:**

    - If several nodes are independent of one another, they may be arranged in various sequences. For example, if tasks A and B can both precede task C, then the sequences (A, B, C) and (B, A, C) represent acceptable topological orders..

Examples of Multiple Topological Orders

Consider a simple DAG with the following edges:

The following mappings are established:

- A is mapped to C
- B is mapped to C
- A is mapped to D
- B is mapped to D

In this scenario, the valid topological sequences are as follows:

- A, B, C, D
- B, A, C, D
- A, B, D, C
- B, A, D, C
- C, A, B, D (this sequence is invalid, as C must follow both A and B)

Implications of Multiple Orders

1. **Flexibility in Scheduling:**

    - In project management or task scheduling, having multiple valid orders allows teams to optimize workflows based on resource availability or team expertise.

2. **Parallel Processing:**

    - Systems that support concurrent execution can take advantage of multiple valid orders to distribute tasks across available resources, improving efficiency.

3. **Algorithm Design**:
    - Algorithms that produce topological orders may yield different results depending on the order in which nodes are processed. This can affect performance and may lead to different execution paths in applications.
4. **Version Control Systems**:
    - In systems like Git, the presence of multiple valid commit orders can result in different histories, especially when merging branches. Each valid order reflects a different possible evolution of the project.

Generating Multiple Orders

- **Kahn's Algorithm and DFS**:
    - Both algorithms can be adapted to generate all possible topological orders. For example, during the queue processing in Kahn's Algorithm, you can explore all nodes with zero in-degrees in any order rather than a fixed order.
- **Linear Time Complexity**:

Both Kahn's algorithm and DFS-based approaches can be implemented to run in linear time, O(V+E)O(V + E)O(V+E), where VVV is the number of vertices (nodes) and EEE is the number of edges.

Flexibility refers to the ability of a system, process, or method to adapt to changes or different conditions. In various contexts, flexibility can encompass several aspects:

1. **Software Development**: Flexibility in software means the ease with which code can be modified, extended, or integrated with

other systems. This can include modular design, the use of APIs, and the ability to support different configurations or environments.

2. **Business Processes**: A flexible business process can adjust to varying demands, changes in market conditions, or customer needs. This often involves scalable systems and agile methodologies that allow for quick pivots.
3. **Work Environments**: Flexible work environments enable employees to adjust their schedules, work locations, or roles to better suit their personal and professional lives. This can enhance productivity and job satisfaction.
4. **Product Design**: Flexibility in product design refers to the ability to accommodate various user needs and preferences, which can involve customizable features or adaptable designs.

In general, flexibility is a valuable trait that can lead to improved resilience, innovation, and responsiveness in both individual and organizational contexts.

Characteristics:

- **Proportional Growth**: The running time grows in direct proportion to the input size (n).
- **Simple Operations**: Often involves iterating through data structures like arrays or lists, performing a constant-time operation on each element.

Examples:

1. **Searching an Element**: A linear search involves examining each element in an unsorted array sequentially until the target value is located or the end of the array is reached.
2. **Copying an Array**: Creating a copy of an array involves iterating through each element and assigning it to a new array.
3. **Finding the Maximum or Minimum**: Scanning through a list of numbers to find the maximum or minimum value requires

checking each element.

Performance:

Linear time complexity is generally efficient for moderate-sized inputs. However, for very large datasets, other algorithms with better time complexity (like logarithmic or sub-linear) may be more suitable.

Example

Consider a simple DAG with the following dependencies:

- Task A transitions to Task B.
- Task A transitions to Task C.
- Task B progresses to Task D.
- Task C progresses to Task D.

A valid topological order for this graph could be:

- A, B, C, D

Use Cases

- **Task Scheduling**:

In project management, determining the order of tasks based on dependencies.

Task scheduling is a critical application of topological sorting, especially when dealing with projects or systems that have dependencies among tasks. Here's an in-depth look at how task scheduling works using topological ordering in Directed Acyclic Graphs (DAGs):

What is Task Scheduling?

Task scheduling involves determining the order in which tasks should be executed based on their dependencies. In many scenarios, some tasks cannot start until others are completed. For example, in software development, a feature cannot be tested until it has been implemented.

How Topological Sorting Applies:

1. **Graph Representation:**

   Tasks may be depicted as nodes within a graph, with the dependencies among these tasks illustrated as directed edges. For example, if the completion of task A is a prerequisite for the commencement of task B, a directed edge would be established from A to B.

2. **DAG Structure:**

   - The structure must be a Directed Acyclic Graph (DAG). This requirement guarantees the absence of cycles, indicating that no task is dependent on itself, whether directly or indirectly.

3. **Topological Order:**

   - A valid topological order of the graph gives a sequence in which tasks can be executed without violating their dependencies. This order ensures that each task is completed before any tasks that depend on it begin.

Steps in Task Scheduling Using Topological Sorting

1. **Build the Graph:**

   - Create a graph representation of the tasks and their dependencies.

2. **Calculate In-Degrees:**

   - Compute the in-degrees for each node. The in-degree represents the number of incoming edges (dependencies) for each task.

3. **Apply Topological Sorting:**
   - Use Kahn's Algorithm or Depth-First Search (DFS) to obtain a topological order of the tasks.
4. **Schedule Execution:**
   - Once you have the topological order, you can execute tasks in that sequence, ensuring that all dependencies are respected.

Example
Consider the following tasks with dependencies:

- Task A is a prerequisite for both Task B and Task C.
- Additionally, Task B must be finalized prior to the commencement of Task D, while Task C must also be completed before Task D can begin
- The corresponding DAG would look like this:

```css
A
/\
B C
\/
D
```

A legitimate topological ordering for this graph may include the following sequences:

• A, B, C, D

• A, C, B, D

Applications of Task Scheduling:

1. **Project Management:**

- Tools like Gantt charts or project management software use topological sorting to schedule tasks based on dependencies.

2. **Build Systems:**
   - In software development, build systems use task scheduling to compile source files in the correct order based on their dependencies.

3. **Workflow Management:**
   - In data processing pipelines, tasks often depend on the completion of previous tasks, and topological sorting helps organize these workflows efficiently.

4. **Job Scheduling in Operating Systems:**
   - Operating systems use task scheduling to manage processes that depend on shared resources or other processes.

Advantages of Task Scheduling with Topological Sorting

- **Efficiency**: Ensures tasks are completed in the most efficient order without delays due to unmet dependencies.
- **Clarity**: Offers a comprehensive outline of task interdependencies, facilitating the management and monitoring of progress.
- **Resource Optimization**: Enables optimal allocation of resources by allowing parallel execution of independent tasks.

Build Systems:

- Ensuring that source files are compiled in the correct order based on dependencies.

- Build systems are essential tools and methodologies that facilitate the automation of compiling and assembling source code into executable applications, libraries, or other deployable components. They are vital in the software development lifecycle, as they handle dependencies, execute tests, and guarantee uniform builds across various environments.

Key Components of Build Systems:

1.Build Automation:

Automates repetitive tasks such as compiling code, linking libraries, and packaging applications. This reduces human error and increases efficiency.

Build automation involves the automation of tasks necessary for the development of software applications, which encompasses compiling source code, packaging binaries, executing tests, and deploying applications. Topological sorting is essential in build automation, particularly when managing dependencies between different components or modules within a project. The following outlines its functionality:

Role of Topological Sorting in Build Automation

1. **Graph Representation of Dependencies**:

In a standard software project, various modules or components often rely on each other. These interdependencies can be illustrated using a Directed Acyclic Graph (DAG), in which:

- Nodes signify modules or tasks.
- Directed edges indicate dependencies (for instance, Module A must be constructed prior to Module B).

2. **Ensuring Correct Build Order**:

    - Topological sorting provides a way to determine a valid build order for the modules based on their dependencies. By producing a linear sequence, it ensures that each module is built only after its dependencies have been successfully built.

Steps in Build Automation Using Topological Sorting

1. Establish Dependencies:

- Recognize all modules along with their respective dependencies. For example, if Module B relies on Module A, a directed edge should be drawn from A to B.

2. Create the Dependency Graph:

- Develop a graph in which each node corresponds to a module, and each directed edge signifies a dependency.

3. **Calculate In-Degrees**:

    - For each module, calculate its in-degree (the number of dependencies it has). This helps in identifying modules that can be built immediately.

4. **Topological Sorting**:

    - Apply Kahn's Algorithm or DFS-based approach to obtain a topological order of the modules. This order indicates the sequence in which modules should be built.

5. **Execute Builds**:

    - Following the topological order, initiate the build process for each module, ensuring all dependencies are met before building dependent modules.

1. **Dependency Management**:

Handles external libraries and modules required by the application. A good build system ensures that all dependencies are resolved and up-to-date.

Dependency management is the process of handling libraries, modules, and other resources that a software project depends on. It ensures that all necessary components are available, correctly configured, and compatible with each other, facilitating smooth development and deployment.

Key Aspects of Dependency Management:

1. **Versioning**: Managing different versions of dependencies to ensure compatibility and avoid conflicts. Semantic versioning (e.g., major.minor.patch) helps indicate the nature of changes.
2. **Resolving Conflicts**: Addressing situations where multiple dependencies require different versions of the same library. Strategies include using dependency resolution tools or creating a unified version.
3. **Transitive Dependencies**: Handling dependencies of dependencies. If a library depends on others, the build system must automatically include those as well.
4. **Lock Files**: Using files (like package-lock.json in npm or Gemfile.lock in Bundler) to record the exact versions of dependencies used in a project. This ensures consistent installations across environments.
5. **Installation**: Automating the download and installation of dependencies, reducing manual setup efforts. Tools like npm, pip, and Maven facilitate this process.
6. **Updating**: Keeping dependencies up to date to benefit from improvements, security patches, and new features while ensuring that updates do not break existing functionality.

Common Dependency Management Tools:

- **npm**: Node.js package manager that manages JavaScript libraries and their dependencies.

- **pip**: The package installer for Python, which manages Python libraries.
- **Maven**: A build automation tool for Java that also handles dependencies through a central repository.
- **Gradle**: A flexible build tool for Java and other languages that provides robust dependency management capabilities.
- **Bundler**: A tool for managing Ruby application dependencies.

Importance of Dependency Management:

- **Simplifies Development**: Automates the process of finding, installing, and configuring libraries, allowing developers to focus on building features rather than managing dependencies.
- **Improves Stability**: Ensures that all required components are correctly installed and compatible, reducing the risk of runtime errors.
- **Enhances Collaboration**: Makes it easier for teams to share projects, as everyone can rely on the same set of dependencies

2. **Configuration Management**:

Allows developers to specify different build configurations (e.g., debug vs. release builds) and manage settings for various environments.

Configuration management (CM) is a critical aspect of managing complex systems and software environments, ensuring consistency, reliability, and compliance across multiple systems. It involves maintaining the state of software, hardware, and system settings over time. Topological sorting plays a key role in configuration management, especially in handling dependencies among various components and configurations. Here's a deeper dive into its significance:

Role of Topological Sorting in Configuration Management

1. **Dependency Management**:

- In numerous systems, the configurations are contingent upon other configurations or services. For example, if Service B requires Service A to be configured prior, this dependency can be represented as a Directed Acyclic Graph (DAG),where:
  - Nodes represent configurations or services.
  - Directed edges represent dependency relationships.

2. **Establishing Correct Configuration Order:**
   - Topological sorting provides a way to determine the correct order to apply configurations, ensuring that each configuration is set up only after its dependencies have been addressed.

Steps in Configuration Management Using Topological Sorting

1. **Identify Configurations and Dependencies:**
   - Catalog all configurations, services, and their interdependencies. This step involves understanding which configurations must be applied before others.
2. **Build the Dependency Graph:**
   - Construct a directed graph representing configurations as nodes and dependencies as directed edges.
3. **Calculate In-Degrees:**
   - For each configuration, calculate its in-degree to understand how many other configurations depend on it.

4. **Topological Sorting:**
   - Use Kahn's Algorithm or DFS-based approaches to obtain a topological order of configurations. This order indicates the sequence in which configurations should be applied.

5. **Apply Configurations:**
   - Execute the configuration changes in the determined order, ensuring that all dependencies are respected.

Example
Consider a system with the following configurations:

- Configuration A (no dependencies)
- Configuration B (depends on A)
- Configuration C (depends on A)
- Configuration D (depends on B and C)

3.Testing:

- Automated tests are incorporated into the build process to guarantee both code quality and functionality. This may encompass unit tests, integration tests, and end-to-end tests.
- Testing represents a vital stage in the software development lifecycle, focusing on the assessment of a system or its components to confirm their proper operation and adherence to defined requirements. The primary objective of testing is to detect defects, uphold quality standards, and validate that the software performs as anticipated across different scenarios.

Types of Testing:

1. Unit Testing: This type assesses individual components or functions in isolation to confirm their correct operation. Typically automated, it aids in identifying issues early in the development cycle.

2. Integration Testing: This testing concentrates on the interactions among integrated components or systems to ensure they function together as intended. It is instrumental in uncovering problems that may occur due to the integration of various modules.

3. Functional Testing: This process verifies that the software operates in accordance with defined requirements. It examines specific features or functionalities from the perspective of the end user.

4. End-to-End Testing: This testing mimics real user scenarios to evaluate the complete application workflow from beginning to end, ensuring that all components operate in harmony.

5. Performance Testing: This type assesses the application's responsiveness, speed, and stability under different conditions. It encompasses load testing (evaluating system behavior under expected loads) and stress testing (assessing performance under extreme conditions).

6. Security Testing: This process identifies vulnerabilities and weaknesses within the application to ensure data protection and adherence to security standards.

7. User Acceptance Testing (UAT): This testing is performed by end-users to confirm that the software fulfills their requirements and is ready for deployment.

Testing Strategies:

- **Manual Testing**: Testers execute test cases manually without automation. Useful for exploratory testing and cases where automation is impractical.
- **Automated Testing**: Uses scripts and tools to execute tests automatically. This is efficient for repetitive tests and regression testing.
- **Test-Driven Development (TDD)** is a methodology in which tests are created prior to the actual coding process. This approach guarantees that the code aligns with the specified requirements from the very beginning.

- **Behavior-Driven Development (BDD):**on the other hand, emphasizes the application's behavior as perceived by the user, fostering collaboration between developers, testers, and business stakeholders.

Importance of Testing:

- **Quality Assurance:** Guarantees that the software is dependable, operates efficiently, and aligns with user requirements.
- **Defect Identification**: Aids in the early detection and resolution of bugs, thereby minimizing the costs and efforts associated with later fixes.
- **Risk Reduction**: Decreases the likelihood of failures during production, safeguarding both users and the organization.
- **Confidence in Releases**: Fosters assurance that new functionalities or modifications will not lead to the emergence of new problems.

3.Continuous Integration (CI):

- Many build systems support CI practices, automatically building and testing code changes as they are pushed to version control, helping catch issues early.
- Continuous Integration (CI) is a software development methodology in which developers regularly merge their code modifications into a common repository, often several times throughout the day. Each integration undergoes automatic verification through the building of the application and the execution of tests, aimed at identifying errors at the earliest possible stage.

Key Features of Continuous Integration:

1. **Automated Builds**: Every code change triggers an automated build process, ensuring that the latest version of the code

compiles successfully.

2. **Automated Testing**: Continuous Integration (CI) systems execute a comprehensive set of automated tests, including unit tests and integration tests, for every build to ensure that the newly introduced code does not cause any bugs or disrupt existing functionalities.
3. **Immediate Feedback**: Developers receive immediate feedback on their changes, allowing them to address issues quickly. This reduces the time spent on debugging later in the development cycle.
4. **Version Control**: CI relies on a version control system (like Git) to manage code changes. This facilitates collaboration among team members and helps track changes over time.
5. **Environment Consistency**: CI ensures that the code is built and tested in a consistent environment, reducing "it works on my machine" problems.

Benefits of Continuous Integration:

- **Early Bug Detection**: CI encourages frequent integration, leading to faster identification and resolution of issues, reducing the likelihood of major defects accumulating.
- **Improved Collaboration**: Developers work on small, incremental changes rather than large updates, making it easier to collaborate and merge code.
- **Faster Release Cycles**: By automating testing and building processes, CI helps speed up the overall development cycle, allowing for quicker releases and updates.
- **Increased Code Quality**: Regular testing and validation of code changes contribute to higher software quality and reliability.
- **Enhanced Developer Confidence**: Knowing that code changes are continuously tested provides developers with confidence in their contributions.

Common CI Tools:

- **Jenkins**: An open-source automation server that supports building, deploying, and automating software projects.
- **Travis CI** is a cloud-based continuous integration service that seamlessly integrates with GitHub, offering automated testing and deployment capabilities.
- **CircleCI**: A cloud-based CI/CD platform that allows for quick setup and integration with various development tools.
- **GitLab CI**: Integrated into GitLab, this tool provides seamless CI/CD capabilities for projects hosted on the GitLab platform.
- **Azure DevOps**: A suite of development tools that includes CI/CD capabilities, supporting various programming languages and platforms.

Common Build Systems:

- **Make**: A classic tool that uses a Makefile to define how to build a project.
- **Gradle**: A modern build tool that uses Groovy or Kotlin for configuration and is popular in Java and Android development.
- **Maven**: Primarily used for Java projects, it uses an XML file (pom.xml) to manage project structure, dependencies, and build processes.
- **Ant**: Another Java build tool that uses XML files to define the build process.
- **CMake**: A cross-platform build system generator that produces makefiles or project files for various IDEs.

Importance of Build Systems:

Build systems are essential in software development, offering a systematic method to automate and oversee the processes necessary for compiling and assembling code into deployable artifacts. The following are several key reasons highlighting the significance of build systems:

1. Automation of Build Processes:

- **Efficiency**: Automating repetitive tasks, such as compilation, testing, and packaging, saves developers time and reduces the likelihood of human error.
- **Consistency**: Ensures that builds are performed in a standardized manner, minimizing variations between development, testing, and production environments.

The automation of build processes represents a fundamental aspect of contemporary software development, facilitating the compilation, testing, and packaging of code into executable applications or libraries. By automating these tasks, organizations can decrease manual labor, reduce the likelihood of errors, and maintain uniformity across various environments.

Key Aspects of Build Process Automation:

1. **Automated Compilation**:
    - The build system automatically compiles source code into binary code, reducing the need for developers to manually run compilation commands. This helps catch syntax errors early.

2. **Dependency Management**:
    - Automated tools handle the resolution and downloading of required libraries and modules, ensuring that all dependencies are included in the build process without manual intervention.

3. **Continuous Integration (CI) Integration**:
    - Automated builds are often triggered by code changes in version control systems (like Git). This integration allows teams to continuously test and validate code as it is developed.

4. **Automated Testing:**

    ◦ Build systems have the capability to automatically execute unit tests, integration tests, and various other automated tests during the build process. This functionality guarantees that new modifications do not disrupt the existing features..

5. **Environment Consistency:**

    ◦ Automation helps maintain a consistent build environment across different stages of development, testing, and production, reducing issues related to "it works on my machine."

6. **Error Reporting:**

    ◦ When a build fails, automated systems provide immediate feedback, detailing errors or failures. This quick reporting allows developers to address issues promptly.

7. **Packaging and Deployment:**

    ◦ After successful builds, automated systems can package the application for distribution and even deploy it to various environments (staging, production) without manual intervention.

Benefits of Automating Build Processes:

- **Increased Efficiency**: Automation significantly speeds up the build process, allowing developers to focus on writing code rather than managing builds.
- **Reduced Errors**: Manual processes are prone to human error. Automation minimizes the risk of mistakes during builds and deployments.

- **Faster Feedback Loops**: Developers receive immediate feedback on their code changes, enabling quicker iterations and improvements.
- **Enhanced Collaboration**: Automated builds create a reliable framework for teams to work together, ensuring that everyone is building and testing the same codebase.
- **Improved Code Quality**: By incorporating automated testing and validation into the build process, teams can maintain higher standards of code quality.

Common Tools for Build Automation:

- **Jenkins** is an open-source automation server designed to facilitate the processes of building, testing, and deploying software applications.
- **Travis CI** is a cloud-based continuous integration service that automates the building and testing of projects that are hosted on GitHub.
- **CircleCI**: A CI/CD platform that automates testing and deployment with a focus on speed and efficiency.
- **GitLab CI**: Integrated into GitLab, providing a seamless experience for CI/CD.
- **Gradle**: A build automation tool that supports multiple languages and integrates well with various testing frameworks.

2. Dependency Management:

- **Simplification**: Build systems manage external libraries and dependencies, automatically downloading and including them as needed.
- **Version Control**: Helps in managing different versions of dependencies, reducing conflicts and ensuring compatibility.

Dependency management plays a vital role in software development, encompassing the organization of libraries, frameworks, and other external elements upon which a project depends. Proper management of these dependencies guarantees that all necessary resources are accurately integrated, compatible, and sustained throughout the entire development process.

Key Components of Dependency Management:

1. **Versioning**:
   - **Semantic Versioning**: Understanding and applying versioning schemes (e.g., major.minor.patch) helps manage changes effectively. Major version changes often indicate breaking changes, while minor and patch versions typically introduce new features or bug fixes.
   - **Version Constraints**: Specifying acceptable ranges for dependencies (e.g., ^1.0.0 or >=1.0.0 <2.0.0) helps ensure compatibility while allowing for updates.
2. **Dependency Resolution**:
   - **Transitive Dependencies**: Handling dependencies of dependencies automatically. When a library relies on other libraries, the dependency management system ensures those are also included.
   - **Conflict Resolution**: Managing situations where different dependencies require conflicting versions of the same library. Tools often provide strategies for resolving such conflicts.
3. **Installation and Configuration**:
   - Automated tools download and install dependencies, configuring them as needed. This simplifies the setup process and reduces the chance of missing components.
4. **Lock Files**:

- **Purpose:**Lock files, such as package-lock.json for npm and Gemfile.lock for Bundler, document the precise versions of all dependencies utilized in a project. This guarantees uniform installations across various environments and among team members.

5. **Updating Dependencies**:

   - Regularly updating dependencies is crucial for security and performance. Tools often provide commands to check for outdated packages and help manage updates while maintaining compatibility.

6. **Documentation**:

   - Keeping clear documentation of dependencies, their versions, and their purposes is vital for team collaboration and onboarding new developers.

Common Dependency Management Tools:

- **npm**: The package manager for JavaScript, managing libraries and their dependencies in Node.js projects.
- **pip**: The package installer for Python, handling libraries and dependencies specified in requirements.txt.
- **Maven**: A build automation tool for Java that manages dependencies through a central repository and XML configuration (pom.xml).
- **Gradle**: A flexible build tool for Java and other languages that provides robust dependency management capabilities.
- **Composer**: A dependency manager for PHP that simplifies package management and versioning.

Importance of Dependency Management:

- **Simplifies Development**: By automating the resolution and installation of dependencies, developers can focus on coding rather than managing library versions.
- **Improves Stability**: Ensuring that all required components are correctly managed reduces the risk of runtime errors and application failures.
- **Enhances Collaboration**: Consistent dependency management across team members ensures that everyone is working with the same versions and configurations.
- **Security**: Regularly updating dependencies helps mitigate vulnerabilities, keeping applications secure and up-to-date.

3. Integration with Continuous Integration (CI):

- **Optimized Processes**: Build systems are frequently connected to CI/CD pipelines, facilitating automated testing and deployment with every modification in the code.
- **Timely Feedback**: Developers obtain prompt insights regarding the quality and condition of their code, which promotes quicker iterations.
- The integration of Continuous Integration (CI) is a crucial element of contemporary software development that improves collaboration, efficiency, and the overall quality of code.
- CI methodologies guarantee that code modifications from various developers are consistently merged into a common repository and subjected to automatic testing, enabling teams to identify problems early and enhance their workflows.

Key Aspects of CI Integration:

1. **Automated Build Processes:**

    - Each modification to the code initiates an automated build process. This guarantees that the most recent code compiles correctly and aids in promptly identifying any compilation errors..

2. **Automated Testing**:
   - Continuous Integration (CI) systems execute a comprehensive set of tests, including unit tests and integration tests, with every build. This process ensures that new modifications do not introduce errors and that the current functionality continues to operate as intended..
3. **Version Control Systems**:
   - CI relies heavily on version control systems (e.g., Git). Developers commit their code changes to a central repository, where CI tools monitor for updates and trigger the build and test processes.
4. **Feedback Loops**:
   - Developers receive immediate feedback on the status of their changes. If a build or test fails, notifications are sent (often via email or messaging platforms), allowing for quick resolution of issues.
5. **Environment Consistency**:
   - CI promotes the use of consistent environments across development, testing, and production. This reduces the risk of "it works on my machine" scenarios, as the CI system typically uses standardized configurations.
6. **Deployment Pipelines**:
   - CI often integrates with Continuous Deployment (CD) practices, allowing successful builds to be automatically

deployed to staging or production environments. This streamlines the release process and ensures that the latest code is always available.

7. **Code Quality Checks:**

   ◦ Continuous Integration (CI) systems may incorporate automated code quality assessments, including linting and static analysis, to uphold coding standards and identify potential problems prior to deployment in a production environment.

Benefits of CI Integration:

- **Early Detection of Issues:** By frequently integrating and testing code modifications, teams are able to identify bugs at an early stage, thereby minimizing the cost and effort required to address them later in the development process.
- **Faster Development Cycles:** CI enables quicker iterations and faster release cycles, allowing teams to respond to user feedback and market changes more rapidly.
- **Increased Collaboration:** Regular integration encourages better collaboration among team members, as developers are constantly merging and reviewing each other's changes.
- **Improved Code Quality:** Automated testing and code quality checks lead to higher standards of code quality and more reliable software.
- **Enhanced Confidence:** Knowing that changes are continuously tested and validated provides developers with confidence in their contributions and in the overall stability of the application.

Common CI Tools:

- **Jenkins:** An open-source automation server that enables developers to establish continuous integration and continuous deployment (CI/CD) pipelines for the purposes of building, testing, and deploying applications.

- **Travis CI:** A cloud-based continuous integration platform that effortlessly connects with GitHub repositories, providing automated testing and deployment functionalities.
- **CircleCI**: A CI/CD platform that automates the development process and integrates with various tools and services.
- **GitLab CI**: Integrated directly into GitLab, offering seamless CI/CD capabilities for projects hosted on the platform.
- **Azure DevOps**: A comprehensive suite of development tools that includes CI/CD pipelines, version control, and project management features.

4. Support for Multiple Configurations:

- **Flexibility**: Build systems can handle different configurations (e.g., debug vs. release builds) and environments (e.g., local, staging, production), making it easy to adapt to varying requirements.

Support for multiple configurations in software development refers to the ability of build systems and deployment processes to handle different environments, settings, and versions of an application seamlessly. This flexibility is essential for accommodating various development, testing, and production scenarios.

Key Aspects of Supporting Multiple Configurations:

1. **Environment-Specific Settings**:
    - Applications often need different settings for development, testing, staging, and production environments. Configuration management allows developers to specify environment-specific parameters (e.g., database URLs, API keys, feature toggles) without changing the core codebase.

2. **Build Profiles:**
   - Build systems can define multiple build profiles or configurations (e.g., debug, release) that adjust compilation options, optimization levels, and included resources based on the intended use case.
3. **Configuration Files:**
   - Many applications use configuration files (e.g., .env files, config.json, application.yml) to manage settings. These files can be easily swapped or modified based on the environment.
4. **Feature Flags:**
   - Implementing feature flags allows teams to enable or disable features in production without deploying new code. This supports testing features in production and rolling out changes gradually.
5. **Conditional Logic:**
   - Build scripts can include conditional logic to determine which dependencies or modules to include based on the configuration being used. This reduces unnecessary bloat and optimizes performance.
6. **Containerization:**
   - Tools like Docker facilitate the creation of environment-specific images, ensuring that applications run consistently across different environments. Each container can be configured for a specific use case.

Benefits of Supporting Multiple Configurations:

- **Flexibility**: Developers have the ability to swiftly alternate among various configurations, allowing them to test and validate their code across multiple environments with minimal rework.
- **Reduced Risk**: Having well-defined configurations for different environments minimizes the risk of introducing environment-specific bugs.
- **Easier Testing**: Teams can easily replicate production conditions in testing or staging environments, leading to more accurate testing and fewer surprises during deployment.
- **Faster Development Cycles**: Developers can work in their local environments while being assured that configurations are correctly set for integration and production, speeding up the development process.
- **Simplified Collaboration**: Clear separation of configurations allows teams to work on different features or fixes without stepping on each other's toes.

Tools and Practices for Managing Multiple Configurations:

- **Build Tools**: Tools like Maven, Gradle, and Make support defining different build profiles and configurations, allowing easy switching between them.
- **Environment Variables**: Using environment variables helps manage sensitive information and configuration settings across different environments without hardcoding them into the codebase.
- **Configuration Management Tools**: Tools like Ansible, Chef, or Puppet can automate the setup of different environments, ensuring that all necessary configurations are applied consistently.
- **CI/CD Integration**: Continuous Integration/Continuous Deployment pipelines can be configured to automatically select the appropriate settings based on the branch or environment

being deployed.

5. Improved Code Quality:

- **Automated Testing:** Many build systems integrate testing frameworks, allowing for continuous testing and ensuring that code meets quality standards before deployment.
- **Error Detection:** Early detection of issues in the build process can prevent bugs from reaching production.

- Enhanced code quality is a primary objective in software development, as it significantly influences the maintainability, performance, and dependability of an application.
- Code of superior quality is more comprehensible, easier to interpret, and simpler to modify, resulting in a reduction of bugs and a more resilient software product.

Key Factors Contributing to Improved Code Quality:

1. **Code Reviews:**

Regular peer reviews help catch potential issues and promote best practices. Reviews encourage collaboration, knowledge sharing, and adherence to coding standards.

1. **Automated Testing:**

Implementing automated tests (unit, integration, and functional tests) ensures that code behaves as expected. This catches bugs early in the development process and provides confidence when making changes.

3. **Static Code Analysis:**

Tools that analyze code for potential issues (such as style violations, bugs, and security vulnerabilities) before runtime can identify problems early. Examples include ESLint for JavaScript, SonarQube, and FindBugs for Java.

4. **Continuous Integration (CI):**

Continuous Integration (CI) practices contribute to the preservation of code quality by executing tests and validations automatically with each code commit. This process guarantees that new modifications do not lead to regressions or disrupt existing functionalities.

5. **Adherence to Coding Standards:**

Following established coding conventions and guidelines improves readability and consistency, making the code easier to understand for all team members.

6. **Refactoring:**

Regularly revisiting and improving existing code (refactoring) helps eliminate technical debt and enhances the overall structure and clarity of the codebase.

7. **Documentation:**

Comprehensive and well-organized documentation, including both inline comments and external references, enhances developers' comprehension of the code's intent and application, thereby streamlining maintenance and onboarding processes.

8. **Use of Design Patterns:**

Implementing well-known design patterns can improve code organization and reusability, leading to cleaner, more efficient code.

Benefits of Improved Code Quality:

- **Reduced Bugs**: High-quality code tends to have fewer bugs, leading to a more stable application and reduced support and maintenance costs.
- **Easier Maintenance**: Well-structured and documented code is easier to modify and extend, allowing teams to implement changes quickly and efficiently.
- **Enhanced Collaboration**: Code that adheres to standards and is well-documented fosters better collaboration among team members, reducing misunderstandings and enhancing productivity.
- **Increased Developer Satisfaction**: Working with clean, high-quality code boosts developer morale and productivity, as it reduces frustration and enhances the overall development experience.
- **Faster Development Cycles**: With fewer bugs and easier maintenance, teams can iterate faster, delivering features and updates more rapidly to users.

6. Facilitating Collaboration:

- **Team Coordination**: A consistent build environment facilitates collaboration among multiple developers on the same project, effectively minimizing compatibility issues.
- **Documentation**: Build files (e.g., Makefile, pom.xml, build.gradle) serve as documentation for the build process, aiding understanding and onboarding for new team members.

Facilitating collaboration in software development is crucial for enhancing productivity, ensuring quality, and fostering a positive team culture. Effective collaboration helps teams work together seamlessly, share knowledge, and deliver high-quality software more efficiently. Here are some key aspects and practices that promote collaboration:

Key Aspects of Facilitating Collaboration:

1. **Version Control Systems:**

Tools such as Git enable numerous developers to collaborate on the same codebase at the same time. They offer features for branching, merging, and monitoring changes, thereby facilitating cooperation without the risk of conflicts.

2. **Code Reviews:**

Regular peer evaluations promote collaboration among team members as they assess one another's code, provide constructive feedback, and engage in discussions about best practices. This process not only elevates the quality of the code but also fosters an environment of knowledge exchange..

3. **Continuous Integration (CI):**

CI systems automate the build and testing processes, allowing developers to integrate their changes frequently. This fosters a shared understanding of the codebase's current state and reduces integration issues.

4. **Communication Tools:**

Utilizing platforms such as Slack, Microsoft Teams, or Discord significantly improves real-time interaction among team members. These tools enable discussions, prompt inquiries, and the exchange of updates.

5. **Documentation:**

Maintaining clear documentation (e.g., wikis, README files, and inline comments) ensures that everyone has access to essential information about the project, reducing ambiguity and improving onboarding for new team members.

6. **Agile Practices**:

Agile methodologies, including Scrum and Kanban, foster collaboration by facilitating regular meetings, such as daily stand-ups, sprint planning sessions, and retrospectives, which ensure that the team remains aligned and concentrated on common objectives.

7. **Shared Tools and Platforms**:

Utilizing collaborative tools (like Confluence, Trello, or JIRA) for project management and task tracking helps teams stay organized and aware of each other's work.

8. **Pair Programming**:

    - This practice involves two developers working together at one workstation. It fosters real-time collaboration, knowledge sharing, and immediate feedback, enhancing both code quality and team cohesion.

Benefits of Facilitating Collaboration:

- **Increased Productivity**: Effective collaboration minimizes duplication of work and streamlines processes, allowing teams to deliver features and fixes more quickly.
- **Enhanced Problem-Solving**: Diverse perspectives lead to more creative solutions. Collaboration encourages brainstorming and collective problem-solving.
- **Improved Knowledge Sharing**: Team members can learn from each other's experiences and expertise, leading to skill

development and a more versatile team.

- **Stronger Team Dynamics**: Collaborative practices foster a sense of ownership and accountability, building trust and camaraderie among team members.
- **Higher Code Quality**: With multiple eyes on the code, issues are caught earlier, leading to higher overall code quality and fewer bugs in production.

7. Simplified Release Management:

- **Automated Packaging**: Build systems can automate the process of packaging software for deployment, ensuring that all necessary files and configurations are included.
- **Versioning**: Helps maintain clear version control and change logs, which are critical for tracking releases.
- Simplified release management is a crucial aspect of software development that streamlines the process of deploying applications and managing software versions.
- By making release management more efficient and less error-prone, teams can deliver new features, updates, and fixes to users more rapidly and reliably.

Key Aspects of Simplified Release Management:

1. **Automated Deployment**:

    - Using Continuous Deployment (CD) practices allows for automatic deployment of code changes to production environments once they pass testing. This reduces manual effort and minimizes the risk of human error during deployments.

2. **Version Control**:

- Maintaining a clear versioning strategy (e.g., semantic versioning) helps teams track changes and manage releases effectively. Each release can be associated with a specific version number, making it easier to roll back if necessary.

3. **Release Pipelines**:

   - Implementing CI/CD pipelines automates the entire process of building, testing, and deploying applications. This ensures that all necessary steps are followed consistently, reducing the risk of overlooked tasks.

4. **Environment Consistency**:

   - Utilizing containerization (e.g., Docker) ensures that applications run the same way across different environments (development, staging, production). This reduces issues related to environment discrepancies.

5. **Change Management**:

   - Keeping track of changes, features, and bug fixes in a structured manner (e.g., using a changelog) provides visibility into what is included in each release, helping teams communicate effectively with stakeholders.

6. **Rollback Mechanisms**:

   - Implementing automated rollback procedures allows teams to quickly revert to a previous version if a deployment encounters critical issues. This ensures higher availability and reduces downtime.

7. **Testing Environments**:

   - Setting up staging environments that mirror production allows for thorough testing before releases. This helps catch issues that might not be apparent in development.

8. **Monitoring and Feedback**:

   - Integrating monitoring tools post-deployment allows teams to gather feedback on application performance and user experience. This information is vital for identifying issues and planning future releases.

Benefits of Simplified Release Management:

- **Faster Release Cycles**: Automation and streamlined processes enable quicker deployment of features and fixes, improving responsiveness to user needs.
- **Reduced Errors**: By minimizing manual steps in the release process, the likelihood of errors decreases, leading to more stable deployments.
- **Increased Confidence**: Knowing that robust processes are in place allows teams to deploy changes more confidently, reducing anxiety around releases.
- **Better Collaboration**: Clear documentation and structured processes promote better communication among team members, ensuring everyone is aligned on release goals and status.
- **Improved User Satisfaction**: Faster and more reliable releases enhance user experience, as customers receive updates and fixes in a timely manner.

8. Enhanced Productivity:

Enhanced productivity in software development refers to the ability of teams to deliver high-quality software efficiently and effectively. This can be achieved through various practices, tools, and methodologies that streamline workflows, reduce bottlenecks, and foster collaboration. Here are key aspects that contribute to enhanced productivity:

Key Factors Influencing Enhanced Productivity:

1. **Automation:**
    - Automating repetitive tasks, such as testing, deployment, and builds, allows developers to focus on more critical aspects of development. Tools like CI/CD pipelines minimize manual effort and speed up the software delivery process.
2. **Version Control Systems:**
    - Employing systems such as Git facilitates smooth collaboration among team members, permitting several developers to concurrently work on various features or bug fixes without encountering conflicts.
3. **Agile Methodologies:**
    - Agile frameworks, such as Scrum or Kanban, promote iterative development, regular feedback, and adaptability. This approach helps teams respond quickly to changing requirements and deliver value incrementally.
4. **Effective Communication:**
    - Tools and practices that facilitate real-time communication (like Slack or Microsoft Teams) improve collaboration, enabling team members to quickly share updates, discuss issues, and coordinate efforts.
5. **Clear Documentation:**

  - Maintaining comprehensive documentation enables team members to grasp the codebase, project objectives, and procedures, thereby minimizing the time required to locate information or resolve misunderstandings..

6. **Integrated Development Environments (IDEs)**:

   - Utilizing robust integrated development environments (IDEs) that offer functionalities such as code completion, debugging, and built-in version control can greatly improve the efficiency of developers.

7. **Code Quality Practices**:

   - Implementing code reviews, automated testing, and static analysis ensures that the codebase remains clean and maintainable, reducing technical debt and simplifying future development.

8. Task Management Tools:

   - Employing project management platforms such as JIRA, Trello, or Asana enables teams to systematically arrange tasks, establish priorities, and monitor progress, thereby ensuring that all members are synchronized with the objectives and timelines.

Benefits of Enhanced Productivity:

- **Faster Time-to-Market**: Efficient workflows and automation enable teams to deliver features and fixes more quickly, allowing organizations to respond to market demands faster.
- **Higher Quality Software**: With a focus on code quality and automated testing, teams can produce more reliable and robust applications, leading to fewer bugs in production.

- **Improved Team Morale**: Streamlined processes and clear communication foster a positive working environment, boosting team satisfaction and motivation.
- **Better Resource Utilization**: By minimizing waste and optimizing workflows, teams can achieve more with the same or fewer resources.
- **Greater Innovation**: With more time to focus on strategic initiatives rather than repetitive tasks, teams can explore new ideas and technologies, driving innovation within the organization.

Focus on Development:

By handling the complexities of the build process, developers can focus more on coding and feature development rather than build-related issues.

Focus on Development refers to creating an environment where developers can concentrate on writing code, solving problems, and delivering features without unnecessary distractions or overhead. This focus is crucial for fostering creativity, enhancing productivity, and ultimately producing high-quality software. Here are key elements that contribute to maintaining a strong focus on development:

Key Aspects of Focusing on Development:

1. **Streamlined Processes**:

    ◦ Simplifying workflows and eliminating unnecessary steps help developers spend more time on actual coding. This can involve automating repetitive tasks and using efficient project management practices.

2. **Effective Tools**:

    ◦ Providing developers with powerful tools (IDEs, version control systems, CI/CD platforms) allows them to work more efficiently. Tools that integrate seamlessly can minimize context switching and keep developers in a productive flow.

3. **Clear Requirements**:
    - Well-defined project requirements and user stories reduce ambiguity and help developers understand what needs to be done. This clarity allows them to focus on implementing solutions rather than guessing or clarifying requirements.
4. **Minimized Interruptions**:
    - Creating a work environment that limits distractions—such as unnecessary meetings, excessive notifications, or unclear priorities—enables developers to maintain their focus on coding tasks.
5. **Encouragement of Best Practices**:
    - Promoting coding standards, code reviews, and testing practices enhances code quality and reduces the time spent on debugging and rework. This allows developers to focus on delivering new features instead.
6. **Collaboration and Communication**:
    - While collaboration is important, balancing it with focused work is key. Establishing designated times for collaboration (e.g., stand-ups, retrospectives) can help minimize interruptions during coding sessions.
7. **Time Management**:
    - Encouraging practices like time blocking or using techniques such as the Pomodoro Technique can help developers

allocate specific periods for focused work, enhancing their productivity.

8. **Continuous Learning**:

    - Providing opportunities for developers to learn new skills or technologies can keep them engaged and motivated, allowing them to tackle challenges more effectively and focus on their development tasks.

Benefits of a Focused Development Environment:

- **Increased Productivity**: When developers can focus on their tasks without distractions, they are more likely to produce high-quality work in less time.
- **Higher Quality Code**: A focus on development promotes thorough testing and code review practices, leading to fewer bugs and more maintainable code.
- **Enhanced Creativity**: With the freedom to explore solutions and implement innovative ideas, developers are more likely to contribute creative solutions to problems.
- **Improved Job Satisfaction**: A supportive environment that emphasizes focused work can lead to higher morale and job satisfaction among developers, reducing turnover and fostering team loyalty.
- **Faster Time-to-Market**: By minimizing distractions and enabling efficient workflows, teams can deliver features and products to market more quickly, improving responsiveness to customer needs.

- **Reduced Downtime**:

Automated builds and tests mean fewer disruptions in the development workflow, enhancing overall productivity.

Reduced downtime refers to minimizing the periods when a system, machine, or service is not operational or available. This can lead to increased productivity, efficiency, and overall performance in various settings, such as manufacturing, IT systems, and service industries. Strategies to achieve reduced downtime may include:

1. **Preventive Maintenance**: Regularly scheduled maintenance to prevent unexpected breakdowns.
2. **Real-time Monitoring**: Using technology to monitor systems and detect issues before they lead to failure.
3. **Employee Training**: Ensuring staff are trained to operate equipment correctly and respond to issues swiftly.
4. **Backup Systems**: Implementing redundancy to keep operations running even when primary systems fail.
5. **Streamlined Processes**: Optimizing workflows to reduce the time needed for repairs and maintenance.

www.ingramcontent.com/pod-product-compliance
Lightning Source LLC
LaVergne TN
LVHW091310150826
845673LV00006B/1606

* 9 7 9 8 8 9 7 4 4 3 7 1 0 *